The One True Cat

The One True Cat

A Memoir with Cats

Chuck Taylor

Genres 4 press

The names of cats and people have been changed. I'm not sure why. It just
seemed the right thing to do, especially for cats, who tend to be more private
than humans.

ISBN: 978-0-9839715-6-6
Library of Congress Control Number: 2012941015

Cover art by Corina Carmona
Manufactured in the United States of America

Four Genres Press
Dallas, Texas

This book is dedicated to Skitzy,
great and happy cat of the woods,
fine companion, warm tent mate,
and excellent hiker along Austin's
Barton Creek trails.

Acknowledgements

Thanks to those who were kind enough to share with me their wonderful cats and their holy cat knowledge: Karen Mal, Turquoise Woman, Janet McCann, Takako Taylor, Lisa Taylor, and Will Taylor. Thanks to A. William Hinson for his expertise with computer programs that helped greatly with book design. I thank those kind enough to send me cat photos to use in this book and who waited so patiently while I recovered from illness. My apologies to those whose pictures the publisher wasn't able to put into the book because of technical problems.

Viva la difference!

The good dog's easy to love.
The good dog does what you say.

The good cat's harder to love.
The good cat goes its own way.
—Chuck Taylor

Preface

Here's a chance to follow a life with cats, a life containing crevices of light and dark, gardens of order and disorder, as well as the good bread of cats and the grit of cats.

You'll get to go on a journey where the soul of a cat meets the soul of the human. You will see not cats separated and alone, but cats living in a world with others.

What you hold in your hands is not a pile of data on cats. It is not a description of breeds. You can get that off the Internet. The book you hold is not a puff ball kind of book, but a true story of the search for love. Whether or not you're a big fan of felines, expect some tears and laughter as you travel this road of words. I expect you will find yourself in some of these pages. Keep in mind this is a memoir, a version of truth the author's memory serves up. Some cats, if they could speak, might remember differently.

Personal Ad:

FAMILY SEEKS THE ONE TRUE CAT

Family seeks perfect cat. Breed, color, or markings are unimportant because the family is mainly concerned with the cat's character. The cat can be large or small, but must be in reasonably good health. The cat must enjoy life inside and outside. The cat should be affectionate but not pushy—no waking people at dawn or in the wee hours of the night. The family expects the cat to "take care of business" outside. The cat must tolerate the dog of the house. The cat should not be a bird hunter, since the family has in the yard numerous bird feeders. As an extra plus—but not required—the cat might enjoy daily strolls. Plenty of love and good food guaranteed. No drugs or alcohol.

1

Last night, an hour before my wife Sayuri and daughter Naomi came home from work, the UPS man rang the doorbell. I had been waiting for the doorbell to sing for two days. By the time I walked from my study to the front door, the brown van was speeding down the block, but directly in front of the door sat a large cardboard box.

I sensed what it was, dragged it over the doorsill onto the living room carpet, and went to get scissors and knife to open the box. The box opened easily, but it took me a while to find the directions as well as the bolts and tools for assembly. They were hidden inside a green bag inside one of the cat hutches.

We'd been waiting a week. Before our order we'd checked a number of stores in town and then done research on the Internet. We were amazed how much prices varied for the exact same item— up to forty dollars, in fact. But now we owned one of those luxury devices—a cat tree! On the Internet we'd read testimonials of happy owners describing how easy the unit was to put together and how their joyous cats got busy scampering on it before fully assembled.

The illustrations on the instruction sheet were poor, and there were no step-by-step directions. Still, after a number of false starts, I got our unit together in a slightly trying forty minutes. The cat tree was covered in green carpet. It had two cathouses, or hutches, and two perches. I carried the cat tree out to the garage and set it right above a set of support legs on the ping pong table. I picked up our gray and white cat with the short tale—Stubby I call him—and set the cat on a perch. Stubby jumped off and fled out the garage door. I got a second cat, Chibi, and stuffed him in one of the hutches. Chibi spun around, jumped, and also fled. I got our third cat, Pounce, from out on the driveway under my pickup, and put him on the highest perch. It was obviously too high. Pounce gingerly rotated around, leaped from the high perch to the low perch, and then to the ping pong table and out the open garage door like the others.

Shortly after my wife and daughter got home, we all moseyed out to the garage to find out if any of the cats were enjoying the cat tree.

It was empty. No cat in sight.

"Maybe it's too high on the ping-pong table," my daughter Naomi suggested. Naomi is a high school senior now. She is a tall and graceful swan and knows everything.

"We need to give them time," Sayuri said, "to get used to it." Sayuri and I have been married nineteen years. We met in Japan in 1991. She is the wise one of the family.

"There's only one constant with cats," I replied, "and that's they

2

will constantly do what you don't expect. They're so cute, so cuddly and playful, when young. What happens when they grow up?"

"Are you still playful?" my wife joked.

"I can be." I laughed. As we headed back to the house, I tickled my wife along the ribs.

"You take a dog," I added. "A dog begins by crying all night, pooping all over the place, and chewing up your shoes, but a dog matures to be man's best friend."

"Here we go again," my swan daughter said.

"I've had near perfect dogs," I continued. "Two of them, in fact, but I've never had a near-perfect cat."

"Maybe it's you and not the cats," my wife replied. "Or maybe it's just your fate."

"One true cat—one long relationship with a compatible cat in my lifetime—that's all I ask."

It's a month later, December 2009, and still none of the cats have discovered the arboreal delights of the cat tree. I've put it on the floor of the garage and I've put it on the front porch, but my hundred-dollar purchase continues to be ignored. Maybe I need to hide small bowls of tuna on the cat tree, or maybe I should pack the gizmo back inside the box and mail it back for a refund.

We bought the cat tree out of guilt, after banishing all cats mostly to the outside world. We had discovered urine stains in places all over the house: on the sofa, on the sides of desks, on my fancy *Condensed Oxford English Dictionary*, on a number of art books, and on the stereo speakers. We hoped our guilt was going to be eased by the cats adventurously exploring all levels of the cat tree. No, what they wanted was inside the house. The heater in the garage, during generally warm Texas winters, was not enough for our sensitive feline gang.

This yearning for the one true cat—where does it come from? I feel like a virginal fifteen-year old mooning for a special someone across the room in a freshman English class. I feel beyond ridiculous. Every mature, sane person knows near perfection on this planet is impossible. Yet I hope and dream. I want a cat that jumps on my lap purring when I get home from work. I want a cat that curls in the corner of the bed to sleep at night. I dream of a cat that plays wrestling games with my dog. Do these yearnings make me an incurable romantic?

The one true cat, the almost perfect cat—is it not human nature to yearn for perfection? Is not the search for perfection a noble human trait? I decided to write this book, a memoir of my life with cats, to glean some understanding and assist me, if at all possible, to either give up on an impossible dream—or locate the right cat. Perhaps that's the one, the one true cat, looking over at me on the next page.

Let me caution readers of potholes up ahead. That's how it runs in life and relationships—up and down—and here the downs that arrive are sometimes funny and sometimes sad. This writer, you will see, can be an incredibly idiotic person, and has a lot of learning to do about what love demands. At times, this writer's a backslider.

2

The dank basement of a Chicago hospital way back in 1947, and in that basement a windowless side office, and in that office a black uniformed security guard who my father has known for a long time. In a back corner of Mr. Seaver's office, half-hidden, rests a wooden box of rags. Snuggling under the rags, four newborn kittens.

"Can I hold one, can I hold one—please, oh please?" I asked Mr. Seaver as he sat shuffling through billing sheets. He'd always been kind to me, letting me pull the cable on the ancient elevator that was only a platform in a vertical tunnel going up four floors in the old section of Presbyterian Hospital.

The elevator was indeed primitive. You needed to clutch your arms to your sides because the counter-weights would whiz down

5

silently along the walls as the platform went up. The security guard was there to guarantee that nothing unauthorized went in or out of the hospital on its old and dangerous elevator.

Ah, but a hospital with kittens! I loved my father's place of work. You could count on surprises around every floor. In an office on the fifth floor in a newer part, a doctor had converted a giant, 19th century glass and metal tank into a fish tank that held giant angelfish. The Presbyterian Hospital was ten minutes from the downtown loop of what was then America's second largest city. This was before the rise of Texas and California, when Illinois was a powerful state.

But the kittens, the kittens! The man in the uniform said I could hold a baby if I was careful not to let the kitten fall.

"They are fragile when small," Mr. Seaver explained. "Their eyes are not yet open."

And so lovely, so furry precious! Each one with a different pattern of colors! What makes the magic of animals for children? I was a boy of four, and I was going to hold in my own arms, for the first time, one of these amazing tiny, furry babies. I would be nurturer. I would be giving love and care to a creature more vulnerable than I was at my small age.

I underestimated how the small one could squirm, and how much the baby yearned to be back in the safety of the wooden womb of a box with its mother. The kitten slipped between my arms and fell two feet onto the concrete floor by my feet, landing on his head.

The kitten's body shook a moment and then lay still. I burst into tears. In my first attempt, I'd failed as a care giver. I'd failed at giving love. My heart felt shattered.

It was my first time to be the cause of the death of another living creature, and it is one of my first memories.

The faces of my father and the man in uniform registered, at first, shock, and then disappointment—but they did not scold. Mr.

Seaver picked up the dead kitten and carried the animal away to another room. My father put his arm on my shoulder and led me away. They knew I had not meant to harm the kitten. They may have felt responsible themselves for giving in to a small child's pleadings.

Those years before school started, I remember locking myself in the bathroom, and my father using a ladder to climb in through the bathroom window to get me out.

I thought he would be furious. I looked down at him, standing on a edge of the tub, as he came up the ladder. But when he got inside he was kind.

I remember the kitchen, the refrigerator with its coil on top, and the ice truck pulling up next door, with the ice man using a big hook to heave the cold block from his truck onto his shoulder, and then the ice man going up and ringing the neighbor's doorbell.

I recall my mother telling me to keep eating my oatmeal and I'd see Mickey Mouse at the bottom of the bowl. I remember the moment I realized it was a trick to get me to eat everything–that it had nothing to do with Mickey–and feeling a little betrayed.

My grandfather would sit at one end of the sofa. I'd sit at the other, and we'd dream the green sofa was a great ship sailing the world. Grandpa would name magical places like Singapore, Tokyo, and Manilla–places he'd either been to or learned about as a unhappy pacifist in the Spanish-American war. Later he became a postman and a perpetual student at the University of Minnesota. He lived close to campus, in the fancy house his father had built with part of the fortune he made in the California gold rush.

And I'd remember the asthma that came July through September from the ragweed, how I coughed and coughed and sucked for air. A steamer boiled at the side of my bed and I stayed alone in my room day after day. The steam made the wallpaper brown and sag in places on the ceiling, and I feared each night that I might not wake

7

in the morning.

One summer I was taken to Presbyterian Hospital, where I had dropped the cat, and put in a bed that was more of a cage with bars on the sides and top. The nurses tied my leg to a rope so I could not reach and burn myself with the steamer at the other end. The days crawled by. I was kept in the bed, except to go to the rest room, and rarely had anyone to talk to. My father dropped by once a day to see me. To entertain myself I untied the huge knot on my leg in a hidden way so the nurses could not see. I tied and untied the knot several times just to have something to do.

By some kind of deep child intuition I was able, even before I started elementary school, to sense that my mother was not quite right. Something was off. I would come up to her when I was bored and ask her what I could do and she would always reply, "I am not your social chairman." I didn't like other kids to visit. Mother threw things at the wall. The only time I got to spend time with her was down in the basement doing the wash. We had a ringer washer that was open at the top. When the clothes were ready she would let me pull them from the water and feed them into the rollers to squeeze the water out. I had to be careful not to get my fingers caught.

Mother seem happiest when my grandpa—her father—was visiting. When he came he slept in a cot down in the basement by a bank of low windows. My sister and I rarely had birthday parties but on my grandfather's fiftieth birthday my mother baked a big cake and put fifty candles on it. The heat was so great the balloons hanging from the ceiling began to pop. I never met my grandmother. She had died giving birth to my mother. I have some of my grandfather's journals and know what a loving man he was.

My sister and I both went to nursery school and kindergarten in nearby Oak Park. When I got to the second grade of elementary school in 1950, I would braid my sister's hair in the morning. I recall in first and second grade being terribly embarrassed when realized

8

I'd forgotten to change and had worn my PJ tops instead of a shirt. All those years we had a spaniel named Susy. I recall Susy next to me on the green sofa, playing the sailing games with grandpa. Susy died a year before we moved to North Carolina. I vividly recall helping my father carry Susy's stiff body down to the basement, then me holding the iron door of our coal furnace, as my father put Susy in for cremation. That was the first time I saw my father cry.

A number of months after Susy died, we got our first cat, a big grey ordinary looking cat who must have been a stray. I'm sure that's why we called him Stray Boy. I remember this cat as being muscular and heavy, but this perception might derive from the fact I was a small child for my age and things seemed big. My father speculated at times that the asthma might have stunted my growth.

Chuck Taylor

3

Not more than six months later, our first cat—the one we called Stray Boy—slipped out a cracked window of the family's blue Plymouth, when we stopped for lunch on a summer day in Ohio. We were moving in 1952 to my father's new job in Chapel Hill, North Carolina. My mother stated, in a matter of fact way, that the cat could never get out the small crack in her car door window. If we did not leave the window cracked Stray Boy would surely get too hot and die.

My mother never apologized for losing Stray Boy. I'm sure she felt bad. It was hard for everyone because we never knew what happened, and that left room for imaginations to soar in dark directions. All Stray Boy wanted, I'm convinced, was to work his way back to our former Illinois home. Hopefully he found a new family.

My sister Jessie and I cried in the back seat until our parents got sick of it and sternly told us to shut up. Dad told us to count down the letters of the alphabet by finding them on the signs we passed. We'd hardly seen poor Stay Boy the whole trip. He'd been cowering under the front passenger seat, panting and occasionally howling.

After that my mother claimed she was allergic to cats, although I never saw her sneeze or develop skin rashes. Three years later my parents decided to depart Chapel Hill, North Carolina, where I'd learned to say "down yonder" and "you chew." I often got beaten up after school for being a "Yankee" while being told to "Save my

11

Confederate money. The South will rise again." I'd actually been at school when the 1954 Supreme Court decision desegregating the schools was announced and remember listening to a confused, flustered principal inquire of an assembly of primary school students if they were willing to go to school with African American kids. (They voted YES! by a wide majority).

What the kids chose in school corresponds with the faith of Nobel Prize winning Mississippi author William Faulkner. He believed that, left to the children, the racial problem of the South would be solved in time, since white and black children grow up playing together. Despite the hopefulness of what happened at school, my mother from Minnesota complained bitterly in North Carolina about the humid heat and the closed in feeling of living in the Blue Ridge Mountains. Daily she yearned for the open Midwest plains. For a year while we lived in the Glen Lennox apartment complex, my family had a black maid. Looking back on it from an adult perspective, it's hard to understand why because my mother didn't work and the apartment was small.

In forth grade, when I was nine in 1952, I remember rushing to get up and dressed for school before the maid came in to wake me. I was skinny self-conscious and did not wish her to see me naked. Some days I went home with the maid—whose name I wish I could recall—and played with her children as she watched over us all. We had a good time playing inside and up and down the street. I don't remember much, but do recall being shocked by the condition of her house and porch. I think in my memory's eye I can see holes in the floor and newspaper glued to the walls.

I asked my dad for an explanation, when he picked me up and we were heading home, but I don't recall him saying anything that put my mind at ease. I do recall seeing signs over drinking fountains indicating which were for white and black. I rode the bus plenty of times in Chapel Hill, but as a child had no awareness of where people sat. Did I too sit at the back of the bus, next to the black women coming wearily home from working in white homes? One of the Glen Lennox neighbors was reputed to be a communist. He was interested in folk music and had a bookstore and record shop in downtown Chapel Hill. We lived in the city during the McCarthy era and I can recall my father pointing out pro-McCarthy signs chalked on highway underpasses.

Although we had no cats of our own during our three years in Chapel Hill, my best friend Slade owned a young orange cat called Shmoo that was a gift from an aunt who lived in the mountains. He named his cat after a character in the Lil' Abner comic strip by Al Capp, popular in the 1950's. In the comic the Shmoos multiplied like rabbits, laid bottles of milk, and fell over dead when you lovingly looked at them. Their meat, when cooked up, tasted exactly like steak.

Slade's Shmoo was a relatively new outside cat belonging to his family. The cat liked to walk with us when we wandered the red dirt roads away from town, through piney woods, searching for ponds to fish in. I noticed, however, that in the four or so months Slade had owned the cat, her behavior seemed to be changing, growing odd. She'd hiss and hunch up her back without any reason, almost as if she did not recognize us when we walked up to give her a pet.

Slade had a sister named Sasha. In the 1950's in the South, during the burning summer months, everyone went around in a pair of shorts, no shoes and no shirt, even the young girls. Mothers felt that their daughters had as yet nothing to cover up. Their chests were flat, exactly like the boys. Few had air conditioning. My father worried we kids might pick up ringworm going barefoot, but all my friends played barefoot outside every day and we were all healthy. The piney woods were all around us, always calling, always there to get lost in.

One Saturday afternoon Sasha was playing with us in Slade's

backyard. We didn't play with her that much, but she was just one year younger than Slade, so she could keep up with many things we did. We were playing red light, a game where one person would count to fifteen, shout "Red light!" and then spin around. If you weren't frozen when the caller turned around, you had to take the caller's place. The first player to reach and touch the caller, after starting out from across the yard, won the game.

Sasha had played the game with us before. Neither Slade or I had noticed that Shmoo the cat was close behind her. Suddenly the feline leaped up and landed on Sasha's naked back, digging her claws in. The cat held the position for a moment, but then her weight, along with Shasha's painful turning and squirming, sent the cat flying off, leaving claw cuts in Sasha's bare skin. Once the cat was off, Sasha ran crying back inside the house for her mother. We followed behind.

Her dad was home and as soon as he saw what had happened, he announced grimly, "We're going to need to get rid of Shmoo."

Sasha's mom was already putting the bright orange Mercurochrome across Sasha's scratched back. She was cooing to her daughter soothingly "It's all right. You're going to be all right."

Sasha was crying, not just from the cuts but from the burning Mercurochrome too. Her mother'd given her a Popsicle to help her focus on something else. I noticed the Popsicle was orange like the Mercurochrome.

Slade was upset. He wasn't saying anything, but I knew he didn't think scratches across a sister's back should mean getting rid of his new pet, his first pet, his only pet. His whole face was turning red. Even his scalp, under his crew cut light brown hair, seemed to take on a pink shade. I thought he might start crying.

"I'm sorry, Slade," his mother said. "I know you love Shmoo. I love him too, but he's showing symptoms of rabies. People could die from rabies if Shmoo were to bite them, and our cat probably has

14

rabies. Your sister's going to be all right. She's lucky. She didn't get bitten."

"Can't we keep him in a cage?" Slade sniffed.

"'Fraid not, son. Rabies turn an animal vicious. Rabies gets in brains and people die. Rabies might could eat your brains too. Has Shmoo ever bitten you?"

"No, I don't think so," we both said, but the truth was we didn't know. We were headed back outside to play, not concerned about small bites, even if they broke the skin. We were determined to play some more and did not want to think unpleasant thoughts.

"I hate to say this to all you kids," Slade's mom said. "You dad's going to need to take Shmoo to a lab in town for tests. Then we'll know more."

"What if Shmoo has rabies?" Sasha managed to ask through tears.

"Well, let's hope not. If the cat has rabies, you're all going to have to get shots. Cats don't get rabies that much."

"I hate shots," said Slade.

"I know you do. We all do, but shots are better than dying," Slade's mother concluded, nodding gravely.

Later the same day Mr. Johnson took Shmoo in a box to the county health department. The tests on Shmoo's brain came back inconclusive, so all three of us children, who had often played with the cat, had to go to the University of North Carolina Medical Hospital for shots. I've blocked this experience from the memory, and would have no knowledge of it if my mother had not told me when I was older. My mother said we got the shots daily.

Slade and I were both nine years old and in the same fourth grade class at school. We'd heard about rabies but had never seen a case. We believed it was something from uncivilized times, maybe fifty years ago, and we thought only dogs got the disease. Not cats,

15

ever. Only dogs contracted rabies in the old movies we saw on TV.

We never saw Shmoo again. Slade never asked his dad why the cat never returned home. We all missed Shmoo. We sensed what had happened, but we didn't wish to hear bad news.

4

In 1954 our family moved back to the same Chicago suburb we'd left, only four blocks away from our former house. Elmhurst was only twenty minutes from the downtown Chicago Loop and had the honor of being a place where the famous poet Carl Sandburg had once lived and written his Abraham Lincoln biographies. We had a small collie named Smiley that I was required to walk each night. Smiley got his name because he was capable of guilt. When he would do something wrong, like sneaking food off the kitchen table, he would begin to smile, even before being caught. The smiling made the collie sneeze and sneeze. We would start laughing at Smiley and poor Smiley would smile and sneeze more.

But the only cat I knew, after the sadness of what happened to Shmoo during our North Carolina years, belonged to a couple that lived a few blocks down the street.

My parents and the Jensens had drunk whisky and played bridge throughout much of World War II at the Randolph Air force Base in San Antonio, Texas. My father and Mr. Jensen had been engaged in research on high-altitude flying. They'd been trying to determine if flying at high altitudes at a low air pressure inside the new bombers being developed was dangerous for the crew. Once the war was over, my family and the Jensen's found themselves living in the same Chicago suburb, with our fathers commuting to work at nearby hospitals. Mr. Jensen became an important figure in the new field of space medicine, a field necessary if astronauts indeed were going to the moon.

The Jensen's cat, named Morgan, was a giant, slant-eyed creature, orange, black, and white, that lived in their double garage amongst lawnmowers, gardening tools, and sports equipment. I'd make friendly kitty sounds entering the dark garage. If I caught a glimpse of slant eyed Morgan, I'd get down on my knees and try to coax him to play by twisting and flipping a small leafy branch on the concrete floor. I'd even come over with an open can of tuna I'd purchased at the I.G.A. grocery with paper route money.

The big animal would pause for a moment, swing its large head around and look at me, and then move slowly into a dim, deep hiding place inside the crowded garage where he could be sure no one could get him. I asked the three Jensen kids if they ever played with Morgan, and they said *no*. If you touched him he'd bite; if you picked him up he'd squirm and you'd get scratched.

So here I'd extended my heart, here I'd brought gifts and asked for a response in return, and the cat turned away. Always Morgan slipped away, from the time I was twelve and we moved back to Elmhurst in 1954, until I was eighteen and went to college in 1961. Over the years I could tell by the look in Morgan's slant eyes that he recognized me, but it was "no-go" as far as he was concerned—no chance that some small trust might develop over time. Cats can be so self-contained. We all know affectionate cats, but I've never known myself a cat to exhibit signs of loneliness.

Like many children I wanted to believe in a gentle, cuddly, Disney Bambi world, but my early experiences with cats—mixed with other life experiences—helped initiate me the process of questioning naive hopes and assumptions. I was wising up a little, beginning to realize that animals have their own good purposes and were not put here to serve people or make them happy. Some may feel I've been cursed when it comes to cats, but my intuition tells me that if people do not candy coat their memories, they will see they've hit plenty of potholes on their life road too.

Yet, why does anyone bother to feed creatures who refuse affections, as cats often do? How are they any different from squirrels or raccoons? Few bother to feed squirrels or raccoons. I never asked my parents' friends the why of cats. I never asked anyone. I should have. What is this strange human fascination with cats? No question, they are sleek, entrancing creatures. I've read that humans tamed most of our domesticated animals, but cats *chose* to live with humans. I know from experience cats can also choose to abandon humans if they find what they consider a better food source or feel compelled to go feral.

Perhaps the Jensen family kept the big cat to chase pesky mice and large rats out of their garage. They were not the kind of family to abuse an animal, although the two older boys were big kids, even when little, and full of the rough and tumble. Maybe their roughhousing terrified Morgan when he was a kitten.

My sister Jessie loved small collie Smiley, but Jessie had grown wary of most dogs. During one summer vacation out west to Yellowstone Park, we spent the first night in a small motel close to the park. The owners of the motel lived on the premises and had a dog chained in a backyard near their apartment. That morning Jessie and I got up and got dressed while our parents slept. They had been driving till late the previous night while we slept in the backseat of the Studebaker station wagon.

Jessie and I went outside, saw the dog and decided to make friends. The dog was a large and seemed to be mostly a poodle. My friend Joey's family owned a poodle back in Elmhurst. He was a frisky, friendly dog. One advantage of poodles, I'd learned, is that they don't shed hairs in a house.

We got down low to the ground and put our hands out to call the dog. I was fifteen, just done with the ninth grade, and my sister was thirteen, in the seventh grade. We made soothing, friendly sounds at the dog and slowly crept forward. The dog looked at us and wagged its tail in a friendly manner. We moved closer on our knees.

The animal abruptly lunged forward on its metal chain. I leaped back in time, but the dog cut my sister with one tooth above her right eye. My parents ended up having to find a doctor to stitch up my sister's wound and did not get to crowded Yellowstone until mid-afternoon. We did locate a camping spot to spend the night. I'll never forget the mother bear that came through the campsite the next morning with her two cubs, turning over garbage cans looking for food. We had no weapons with us, and our only defense would have been to jump in the station wagon and drive away with the tent still attached. Perhaps this second incident added to my sister's fears. We both wisely learned to temper our childhood trust of all animals. Yes, real animals are not Disney cartoons. Dogs and cats can begin to teach us this important lesson.

When Jessie's wound healed, the dog bite left a small groove of a scar on the upper right side of her eye that came to bother her in adolescent years. My parents claimed it gave her face character, and I honestly felt it was not much of a disfigurement. She had been fortunate that the dog had not caught her directly in the eye. When in her twenties and on her own, however, Jessie, working as a secretary in Boston, saved the money to have plastic surgery on the scar, and today you see no sign of it. She now works in counseling.

I mention this unfortunate incident my poor sister suffered because she has never tried to keep a dog or a cat at her place. The event influenced her greatly and she's still uncomfortable around people's pets. To be fair to cats, one should note the obvious—that most cats are small and incapable of doing the damage dogs can do. Cats often have a 'You leave me alone, I'll leave you alone,' attitude. A cat will warn you with an unhappy meow if you swoop him up and he is not ready. Cats generally are low maintenance animals. Just feed 'em and they're happy. Maybe size and less opportunity for trouble leads many women to prefer cats to dogs. Perhaps the domesticity of cats appeal to women. I can't count all the troubles I've almost gotten into with dogs, walking down my neighborhood street or out camping at a nearby state park. Some folks think it fine to leave their dogs untied and outside while they sleep in tents. I always put my dog in the car for the night.

Dogs have been off leash and run up to my dog growling and with teeth showing when I've been walking down a residential street or at a local park. I now carry a walking stick. So far I have never had to strike a dog, but I've had to do plenty of waving. One time I got off my bike to visit a friend. A large aggressive dog appeared out of nowhere and charged me. I fended him off using my bicycle as a shield, calling loudly for the owner to come outside and tie the dog up. Blessed be that cats never present that kind of threat.

Given all the things I've seen happen, I don't know why I'm still crazy about dogs and cats. I'm a hopeless dreamer. Something deep inside the psyche keeps calling. Humans, cats, dogs—we've been together and loved each other for millennia. I've craved the love of animals always—almost as much as, when alone and single, I've longed for a woman.

Chuck Taylor

5

Now my first wife Eileen and I, when we were twenty and newly married in November of 1964, moved into what was said to be the oldest apartment building in Evanston, built in 1895. Evanston was the first suburb north of Chicago, and we lived a few blocks from the borderline separating the two cities. Our apartment was in a converted section of the building's basement. The main attraction was the rock bottom rent of one hundred and fifty dollars a month. The apartment had brick walls painted white and large pipes running along the ceiling barely above our heads.

Eileen's parents, down for a visit from their unincorporated village two miles from the Wisconsin border, were shocked when they walked in our place. I found it, in contrast, beatifically Bohemian. My wife Eileen was a beautiful petite lady with red-black hair and creamy skin. She'd grown up in the tiny village with three brothers and two sisters. As a young woman Eileen was quiet and never said much about our odd apartment. I think she saw it as a necessary early step in every young couple's life.

The apartments came furnished with dark 1940s furniture that suggested a kind of faded stateliness, a charm from an era when a middle class began to have a little disposable cash to buy fine things and were thrilled.

Still Eileen, like her parents, was not overly enthusiastic about our first home. She complained about the expense of the large sheets and blankets we had to purchase when I pushed the two single beds together to make a newlywed's impromptu king sized bed. In the morning the janitor would wake us from the other side of our thin bedroom wall, shoveling chunks of black coal into the furnace.

Our bedroom seemed designed to be dusty. You could taste the coal dust at the back of your throat. Still, we were the first in the whole building to warm up.

We had windows, small ones—two if I remember—on the outside east wall. While lying late in bed on a Saturday morning, we could look up into a small park adjacent to the building and watch pre-schoolers play excitedly on swings and slides. We'd catch sight of the legs of mothers dangling contentedly from benches.

When I washed dishes I could look into the airshaft that ran up the center of the building. It was dark, dusty, and devoid of life. Not even the apartment mice liked the place. By getting down on my knees I could peer up the airshaft and see most of the other apartment windows in the small building, but except for ours they were all painted over with white paint.

We had been given two expensive show cats—a gift from the woman my father was dating after his divorce a year earlier. My mother had moved to California to live near her sister. All this happened quickly following my mother's second suicide attempt and second stay on the psychiatric ward at Evanston Hospital where my father now worked as a pathologist. I worked as a lowly maintenance man while attending college, and my wife Eileen worked as a newly graduated nurse on a medical floor.

I would sit in the living room studying. It was my senior year in college and I was growing nervous about getting into graduate school. The two expensive Siamese—Shady and Shay we called them—would climb up on the back of the old sofa, then inch toward me, one from each side, as I sat in the middle. In a half hour a Siamese would be sitting on my left and right shoulder, and then, at the same time, each would try to creep on top of my head. Not surprisingly, the space was too small for both Shady and Shay.

24

They'd start hissing and I would begin to feel claws extending, starting to dig into my shoulders and scalp as they peered at each other over the top of my skull.

Why did the Siamese attempt this? What on earth was going through their minds? Was it because:

    1) My head was the highest point in the room?

    2) My head was the warmest point?

    3) My head they considered the safest point?

    4) They liked the feel of human hair?

    5) Or maybe they were in competition?

They seemed like the American astronauts and the Russian cosmonauts competing to reach the moon first to prove their superiority.

I would take the two cats down and put them on our bed where they could enjoy the sunlight streaming in the windows, but the ancient bedroom door did not shut all the way. In five minutes the cats would paw the door open and return to the living room to repeat the same couch-to-shoulder-to-head routine. After about five more rounds of this behavior, I'd grow furious and start tossing them across the room. I couldn't put them in the hall or outside. We lived in a crowded, big-city apartment, neighborhood.

They'd always land nimbly on their feet. I did not have the heart to wind up like a major leaguer and pitch them in a crazy fastball against the brick wall. They'd claw my arm to shreds. I thought of making some kind of cage outside, but our old apartment building had no back or front yard. It didn't even have an alley.

For a month I tolerated the head-climbing obsessions of Shady and Shay, but I knew if I didn't do something soon I'd flunk the courses I needed to ace. I was getting way behind on the reading. Eileen and I lived four blocks from Lake Michigan and in my worst moments I half-considered walking out on one of the concrete breakwaters and dropping the two Siamese into the cold water in a sack. That was a common, if terrible, method used by many to get rid of cats in the not too old days, before World War II.

My other horrid fantasy was to go up on the roof of our apartment building. That was easy to do—there was an unlocked door that opened onto the roof at the top of the inside stairway. I could take the Siamese up there, holding them both by the scruff of their necks as one does rabbits. With one in each hand I'd drop them down the building's air shaft. Getting the air shaft door open would be a challenge without losing control of the Siamese.

The fall itself would kill the cats, I figured. If the smell of their deaths began to infiltrate our apartment, I'd tell my wife Eileen it was the odor of dead rats. I could pull open the window above the sink while Eileen was at work, and shovel the two Siamese into garbage bags and put them in the trash out back.

The reason I was interested in the latter horrid mode of murder was because of a story a friend from work had told me. In the old days, the farmers in Europe would drop a live cat from a church's bell tower. If the cat landed on its feet, the farmers would have a good harvest. If the cat landed on another part of its body—yet survived—that meant a difficult year. If the cat died in the drop, that indicated crop failure by blight, by drought, or by sorcery. The farmers, I hope, chose small churches with low bell towers for their cat forecasting.

Yes, I had grown to detest those two Siamese. I was a scholarly young man, but like any young man full of piss and vinegar. Their very look seemed evil and seemed to be pulling evil out of me. No wonder cats traveled with witches in the old folk tales. Shady and Shay were unteachable and in my worse moments I wished for an end to them. Tell me, reader, have you never entertained such dark thoughts? Often I had to stop them oddly sniffing and nibbling on the frayed electric cord attached the old brass lamp I read by in the living room. Yes, murder, riding the world of black magic, was often my fantasy, but of course it was not what I finally ended up doing.

Instead I took them back to my father's small house along the CTA commuter tracks, put the nasty cats inside while he was at work, and called him later in the day about the problem. When I told my father the story of the head-climbing Siamese, I wasn't sure my dear old dad, so patient of my failings, quite believed me.

"Give them back to your girlfriend, please," I begged. "I know they cost a lot of money. She can take them back to the wholesaler and get her money back. I can't stop them from trying to get on top of my head while I'm studying, and I don't think any circus will hire the three of us as a comedy act. I'm going to drown them or wring their necks. They're driving me bonkers!"

My father must have thought me both an ungrateful jerk and

nuts to boot—yet he could sense the anger in my voice and got rid of them.

As a young man I did not have a good image of Siamese cats. Perhaps it was the Disney animated film, *Lady and the Tramp*, where the two evil Siamese plot against the gentle feminine Spaniel, Lady, in their song, "We are Siamese if you please; we are Siamese if you don't please." I suppose 1950's cold war Chinese bigotry lies inside that song. People forget that until President Nixon the Chinese communists were our enemies. Just think of the exaggerated slant eyes the illustrators gave the Siamese in that film.

6

Eileen and I made a second effort to keep a cat; this time it was a gift of what looked to be an American wirehair from a nurse at the large hospital where Eileen worked. Nurses I've found often are insomniacs from the swing shifts they have to work and may at times drink too much in an effort to relax and fall asleep, but they're almost always wonderful folk, the nurturing kind who may at times need to give away extra dogs or cats. When the nurse brought the cat over to our small apartment, she explained that all outside cats actually yearn to be inside house cats.

Eileen and I had moved from Evanston to Iowa City in the autumn of 1965. We made a new home in married student housing across from the city park. I used to stroll around the park to get some exercise and visit with a lone buffalo in a small round enclosure. The buffalo's a herd creature and this fellow looked incredibly depressed and lonely. I called the city's park office about the animal. Apparently a number of city residents complained because a year later the buffalo was sent to a herd in Nebraska.

The nurse who gave us the wire hair worked with Eileen in the state hospital's ICU unit. The cat was a cute little guy and loved to play. We kept him inside our second floor apartment. The nurse had assured us many times that the kitten's mother and his siblings were inside cats. They had never seen the outside world. Our kitten was lonely at first but we played with him whenever we could and he seemed to feel better. The wirehair—we called him George—loved to play with the floor to ceiling drapes, gold colored, that Eileen bought to spruce up our apartment. Sometimes he'd climb five feet up the drapes, get stuck, and meow to get helped down.

The mid-sixties were interesting times to be in Iowa City, once the capital city and now the location of its main university. At the Memorial Student Center in October 1965 I listened to the student Stephen Smith speak at an anti-war demonstration on the immorality of the Vietnam war, and then watched him quietly set fire to his draft card and burn it. Quietly an FBI agent bent down with a small dust pan and whisk broom to sweep up the ashes. Why, I had always wondered, was I carrying around in my wallet that stupid card? How could the US government require a person by law to carry a piece of paper that wasn't a license? The draft card was not a license, unless you thought of it as a future license to kill. No one ever asked me to see my draft card. If they were going to draft me they'd send me a letter. I saw the card requirement as a subtle method of big brother intimidation.

More and more I was turning into an angry young man, so disgusted with the federal government I eventually made a separate peace, burning my draft card in an ash tray at my apartment, muttering to the walls that the Vietnam war was an undeclared and racist war in an obscure place. I would not fight in it. I was practical and cynical. If by rare chance a government official, say a policeman, asked me why I didn't have my draft card in my wallet, I could say I lost it. No FBI agent was around to sweep the ashes out of my ash tray. I dumped them in the trash and told no one, not even my wife Eileen.

When my MA degree was finished in 1966, Eileen decided she wanted to pursue a BS in Nursing. We needed to move back to our home state to take advantage of in-state tuition, in order to be able to afford school for both of us. Northern Illinois was the only place that offered both a degree in nursing and a PhD in English. In January of 1967 we packed up our belongings in the tan Chevelle my father had given us, and pulling a U-Haul, we drove slowly from Iowa City to Dekalb on treacherous icy roads after a snowstorm. I drove slow to prevent the U-Haul trailer from fish-tailing. It took us seven hours to reach DeKalb. Normally the trip would take three and a half. George the wirehair hid the whole trip under the passenger side front seat. He did not let out a peep or a howl. George clearly deserved high marks for being a superior cat in the traveling department.

We were going to move again in Dekalb in about six months, and knowing that cats tend to be territorial, we decided to continue to keep George inside so that when we moved it would be from one inside space to another, and less traumatic. George, we'd been told, was meant to be an inside cat. My hope of a good future with cats was renewed. I put in the back of my mind the unfortunate experiences with the two Siamese in Evanston. George the wirehair was an attractive cat, with stripes of brown, black, and white. He was quite a vocalizer, and would meow plaintively and softly standing next to his food dish when he wanted to be fed. If you picked him up too fast and turned him on his stomach in your arms to give him a hug and kiss, he would let out one sharp meow to tell you he wasn't pleased.

Our second home in DeKalb was a two-room apartment in a large house. DeKalb, fifty miles from Chicago, was then a shabby town with a rundown business district and an impermanent looking college campus made of modernistic buildings that resembled shower stalls. DeKalb was famous for its hybrid corn, and for a man named Glidden who was supposedly perfected the barbed wire that won the West. It was also known for being the headquarters of the Wurlitzer Organ Company.

The son of the company president, Rudolf Wurlitzer, wrote the first LSD novel. Born in Texas, Rudolf Wurlitzer is now a Buddhist. His celebrated cult novel is called *Nog* and was given to me by the renowned Russian cellist, Raya Garbousova, who generously retired

31

from most of her international touring and married Dr. Kurt Biss to live in DeKalb and be a stepmother to his children. This cultivated Russian-Austrian-American family lived in a fine old house full of books and Picasso prints on the main highway through town. They gave me my first real exposure to art and culture.

While in DeKalb Eileen and I had our first child Parker. He was an unplanned baby. Eileen was excited, although I had doubts how we'd manage on our low income. Coming from a troubled family, I did not consider myself father material. We had no health insurance and had to pay for the delivery ourselves. We'd heard many stories growing up about jealous cats sleeping across babies' faces and perhaps semi-intentionally smothering a child, but our nurse buddy back in Iowa City assured us over the phone that these tales were myths. We were twenty-five years old and nervous, not yet sure of what we were doing as parents and not fully aware of the responsibilities we'd taken on.

Our son Parker was actually spending much of his time in his crib in our small bathroom because he had severe colic. Parker was an energetic, blond haired, blue eyed baby, a handsome fellow who from day one had to be up and moving around, but his long bouts of crying, which we rarely could get to stop, went on at times for hours and drove us insane with anxiety. To escape the nailbiting stress of his screaming, we'd shut Parker in the bathroom, shut the bedroom door that led to the bathroom, and then turned the stereo up loud in the living room. With the bathroom door tightly shut the baby was safe from the cat George. We knew that George was uninterested in a screaming baby but were not sure what would happen when our boy fell asleep.

If you think it's a cruel way to treat a screaming baby, you don't have much knowledge of colic. Our pediatrician had recommended putting Parker in a safe place so we could get away from the yelling. With baby Parker in the bathroom, we'd calm down and regain sanity. He'd eventually cry himself to sleep. In 1969 there existed no special medical clinics to help parents cope with colic. Doctors didn't know much about the condition. From reading around and listening to NPR news reports, I'm convinced they still don't know that much.

Our wirehair George was no longer a kitten and now was developing his own strong personality. George became the first cat in my life that I both loved and genuinely respected. Fully grown and quite large, George's main goal seemed now to be to get out of our two room apartment. Space for the four of us was small, so I could relate. George yearned to be FREE. So much for the claim that all inside cats delight to remain inside cats! We called the cat George because he seemed so normal but now we needed to put George on a leash when one of us was going out the door, to restrain him from dashing down the hallway into the back kitchen where the back door might be open, or up the stairs to the second floor. Neither was a route with a guarantee to the outside, but George would try both over and over. Catching George and getting him back into our apartment could take over an hour. I used a large, heavy-ply towel so as not to get scratched.

One day I came home in the late afternoon. Eileen was still at work and our son was at the sitter's. Our apartment was in an old house that had been divided into one-room apartments that were rented solely to Chinese students—I am not sure why. We got our small efficiency apartment free for managing the place, which meant sweeping and mopping the floors as well as collecting rents.

I'd left the one window we had in the bedroom cracked open. Somehow George squeezed through the crack and got between the window and the screen. George must have worked on that heavy ply screen for hours. He managed to create a slit where the screen was attached at the bottom to the black wooden frame. The cat worked on the slit, using his paws, his teeth perhaps, and his weight. Eventually George got the slit long enough and wide enough to wiggle his way out and disappear.

George earned what he wanted, a chance to make it in the real world full of risk and delight. We drove around the neighborhood a couple of days in an effort to locate our lost cat, but I felt no deep remorse when we failed to find him. I pictured George happily raiding the garbage cans of students up and down alleys in our neighborhood. Students it seemed rarely finished their plates of food, or their perpetually ordered pepperoni pizzas. George would discover plenty of tasty morsels to eat.

I was rather pleased for George.

Eileen was not that pleased. Maybe her sense of responsibility, or nurturing, was more developed than mine. Perhaps building the nest was foremost in her heart. Dreams of freedom and adventure, once graduate school was happily over, dominated my dreams.

7

After the loss of cat George we stayed clear of cats for while and planned instead to get a dog when we had larger space. The world was changing. Assassinations had cut the country to its core. In 1968 Martin Luther King had been assassinated on the balcony of the Lorraine Hotel in Memphis, Tennessee. Before Dr. King, President Kennedy, Robert Kennedy, and Malcolm X had been assassinated. Everything seemed to have moved way beyond crazy.

Soon we'd be moving to Texas. I'd landed a job even though my PhD was not complete. My family had lived in San Antonio and Seguin while my dad was stationed at Randolph Air force Base, but I was too small to remember much of those times. What I knew of Texas came from cowboy movies and the reports on television when President Kennedy was killed in Dallas, and then his killer Lee Harvey Oswald was shot by the owner of a strip club, Jack Ruby, in the basement parking area of the city jail.

A month before we were to move from DeKalb, a man slammed into our Chevelle driving the wrong way on a one way street while drunk. Eileen had just loaded laundry from the Dekalb Laundromat into the Chevelle. Our baby son sat strapped in the car seat in the front. Car seats were much more primitive back then but this one did its job and saved our child from many cuts and bruises.

By the grace of God or fortune, both my wife and child received no single injury, but our car got smacked up on both sides. The drunk driver had smashed one side and pushed the other side into a high curb. An alert passerby memorized the license plate number and saw a student sticker on the car's back window. Through the campus police, we were able to locate the man and have him arrested for hit and run. It turned out the fellow was on parole from Joliet prison. He had no insurance, but in court he did pay us two thousand dollars, what the body shop estimated the repairs would cost. I'll never forget seeing the man and his girlfriend striding down the sidewalk arm in arm in celebration after the trial. He wasn't through with the courts of course. She was a lovely young woman. I wondered what heartache the future had in store for her. I hope the heartache turned good. Some women prefer outlaws.

Amazingly the doors of the Chevelle opened and closed, and the windows went up and down. What an great vehicle my father had given me. I loved its red interior and its powerful V-8 engine. An old friend advised me to save some of the money for any possible dangerous hidden damage and not to worry about outside appearance. We had the Chevelle checked over and repairs done. The repairman told us the car was safe.

We pulled a heavy U-Haul trailer behind our crumpled looking car from DeKalb, Illinois, to San Angelo, Texas, without a single hitch—a trip of over 1,100 miles. We felt fortunate to have no cat with us. The baby was enough. We'd seen recently the movie *Easy Rider*, where the main characters Captain America and Billy get murdered on their motorcycles by a southern cracker wielding a shot gun that he pulls from his gun rack. Remembering the assassination of Kennedy in Dallas, I put an "America: Love it or Leave it" sticker on the back of my crumpled car. When we got to Texas we saw plenty of gun racks.

We pulled into San Angelo noticing large billboards all over telling everyone to PRAY FOR RAIN. A drought, I guessed, must be decimating central West Texas ranching and farming. I had never been in a drought. We passed by a giant church on a hill that dominated the landscape.

"That must be the Catholic Church," I said to Eileen.

When we got close we saw that it was a denomination I'd never seen in the Midwest, the Church of Christ. One of my colleagues at my new teaching job said he'd been a minister in the church at sixteen. We unpacked our belongings at married student housing. Both students and faculty lived in the apartments. Our first floor apartment, a two bedroom place, was the largest space Eileen and I had ever lived in, but the college had a rule: no pets. The people in the area were much more conservative than we were used to, but we ended up liking the wide spaces, the mild winters and the great light. I took up photography. Eileen stayed at home and we had a second child, Sebastian. This boy had hair and skin exactly like his mother. Sebastian was quiet and spent his early childhood following his older brother around, trying to do everything he did.

I began working on an underground newspaper at the off campus Newman Center, but when a wealthy donor threatened to shut down the complete Newman Center, we closed the paper. A colleague's daughter wanted to hold an anti-war demonstration, but could find not a place in the whole town that would allow her to hold such an event. Finally, the church across from San Angelo's famous lily pad garden agreed to let the demonstration to go on one weekday night, after dark, in their parking lot. For social life we spent a great deal of time with members of the small Unitarian Fellowship, and I also befriended an Italian sculptor who was writing a book on John Steinbeck and completing a sculpture for the Hemphill-Wells department store downtown. The department store has been closed now for a long time, but the relief sculpture still looks great.

We later bought a house close to the college campus so I could walk to work. Eileen realized that being a stay at home mother was not for her, and took an ICU nursing job. We had a busy life with two small children and both of us working. We did not feel ready for another cat. We hired a woman as a home babysitter who had excellent references. After a three days with her taking care of the kids from ten to three each day, I noticed that both boys were more clingy than usual. On the forth day I went out the front door with my briefcase supposedly headed for work, but instead I went up the driveway at the side of the house and into my converted garage office in the back yard.

I peered out a window for about ten minutes. I saw the woman push my two sons out the back door. She had a stick in her right hand that she raised and pointed at the boys. I guessed what the stick was for, to slap them where it hurts, between the two legs. I remembered my grandparents talking about that discipline method. "Switching" it was called but my grandparents never used the technique. I had learned recently that physical punishment was an accepted practice in Texas public schools. I went in the door and immediately fired the woman. She called me a "damn Yankee" and said my kids were undisciplined brats. I considered summoning the police, but with no marks mercifully on my boys any legal charge I made would have been her word against mine. I didn't say much to counter her anger—just that she could expect no references from us.

We lived in San Angelo from 1969 to 1973. These indeed were interesting times. The Vietnam War continued to rage. I got a summons from my draft board in Chicago and had to drive up there to take a physical, which I failed due to varicose veins in my right leg. We felt isolated in conservative West Texas. We were expected to go to church and attend the college's football games. The dean told me that if I was a famous eccentric like Buckminster Fuller the college might put up with me, but I wasn't famous at twenty nine. I got tired of hearing one person ask a second person about a third person, "Are they a good Christian?" Good Christian meant you were either Southern Baptist or Church of Christ. The two denominations quarreled over whether a single passage in the bible did or did not forbid musical instruments in church.

I suddenly quit my teaching job the summer of 1973 and we moved four and one half hours east to the city former Senator Ralph Yarborough called the Paris of Texas–Austin. My wife drove the Chevelle with the crumpled side panels, the boys in the back seat. I moved our stuff this time in a larger U-Haul truck. Late on a Saturday we pulled into a facility for troubled adolescent boys on HW 183 where our best friends, Alice and Rich—who'd left San Angelo six months earlier—now worked as counselors. My wife and kids were in the car. I looked out the U-Haul truck and saw black smoke coming from under the Chevelle's hood.

I reached across the cab of the truck and quickly cranked down the passenger side window. "Get out! Get out! Fire! Fire!" Eileen squinted and gave me a funny look. I'm not sure if she heard me or saw the flames herself.

I jumped out of the truck cab and raced around the back of the U-Haul to the Chevelle. Eileen was out of the car, pulling the boys out of the backseat. We didn't know if the car would explode, as you see happen in the movies, so we raced inside the building looking for our friends and a fire extinguisher.

We found our friends in the back of the building. My friend Rich called the fire department. I could find no extinguisher however and by the time the truck arrived at the facility the car was burned beyond salvaging. The flames never reached the gas tank in the back, but they had gotten into the interior and burned much of the red seat fabric. About three months later I heard on the local news that our model of Chevelle had been recalled by General Motors for a faulty fuel pump. I've never claimed to be a person spared by grace. Too many good people have bad luck and accidents. Still, I know when it is time to be mindful and say thanks.

Many of our friends had been aghast that we could drive around in a car with crumped side panels. Eileen and I weren't trying to be different. We loved the Chevelle and didn't care how it looked as

39

long as it ran well. The Chevelle was always easy to spot in a parking lot. I've long been comfortable not being obsessed with what other's think. I learned the attitude from my father, the doctor, who commuted into Chicago six days a week in a car he'd gotten in trade for an electric coffee pot. In that roadster the floors were so rusted you could catch the bright shine of street pavement rushing by. Eventually he and I reinforced the floor with plywood. The next car my father bought was a Volkswagen. He was not satisfied with the strength of its bumpers, so we cut old tires for the front and back, unrolling them and wiring them down.

Eileen and I remained in Austin two years, lived in two locations, and stayed away from cats. I worked two jobs part-time—one for the Austin Public Library, the other as a self-employed children's magician—but mostly I stayed at home to write while taking care of our sons. A lot of landlords are not fond of dogs and cats. I've been a landlord myself since and know why. You can clean the carpets and paint the walls after your tenants leave, but still the smells linger. Being something of a house husband in Austin was a grand experience. I got to bond closely with my two little boys Parker and Sebastian. I took them south of the Colorado River to ride the kiddie train and to play on the old fire engine in the children's play scape area.

We also enjoyed going further south on Congress Avenue almost to Ben White, where the Catholic university Saint Edwards is located. Saint Edwards has a castle like central building constructed out of stone in the nineteenth century. It sits on one of the highest hills in Austin, and if you climb to the top of the building you can look out over the green and rolling hills of most of the city. You can see the capital building and the famous UT tower where former Marine Charles Whitman made war on his fellow students on the University of Texas campus in 1966, murdering first his wife and mother at home, and then thirteen from the tower.

I was getting my poems and stories published in magazines and doing some readings that paid, but writing brought nothing near a living wage, so Eileen and I both got to work and eventually found jobs in far West Texas, out in El Paso, where we hoped we might settle down. Still I had itchy feet, the hunger for experience. Would I always be a roamer? Roaming is hardly the way of cats.

I had discovered, much to my surprise, that living in Texas had made me a happier person. As a thin person I preferred the mild winters that prevail in much of the state. Today I never miss the snow, the ice, or the freezing temperatures of the Midwest, although I do miss the people. Chicago seemed grey and overcast half the time. It felt like living inside a small metal pot with a heavy lid. Others don't react that way, but nowadays some northerners, to overcome depression, get up early in the morning to sit in front of a bank of bright lights. The amazing light and the big skies of the Southwest made me more outgoing and optimistic. Even though cats rarely pant, except when they are very frightened, they seem to be able to handle well the heat of Texas. The fact that they drink so little liquid suggest an origin in the deserts of Africa.

When Eileen finished her MA degree in Austin we headed for El Paso in late August 1975. We'd fallen in love with the "Paris of Texas," but the job situation there in the 1970's was highly limited. Austin then was a minor southern city, not the computer and musical place of opportunity it is considered today.

Chuck Taylor

8

El Paso is a dandy place for those who love the desert. The topography of the land makes the place special. You have open vistas to expand your spirit outward across the desert flats, and you have, paradoxically, mountains—the Franklin chain to be exact—cutting right into the city, lifting your eye up into the grand and transcendent. Mountains in the past, when I lived in Chapel Hill, made me feel claustrophobic—closed in—but not the Franklins. Every day the mountains take on different hues depending on the position of the sun in the sky. There were springs up high in the mountains I loved to hike to.

Beyond topography El Paso gives you a mix of cultures and people. I met people of all kinds, and still count as friends painters, poets, musicians, a historian-activist, and a sculptor. Many have a deep loyalty to their city and can't imagine living anywhere else. I worried that the desert city of El Paso would make us feel alienated as the desert town of San Angelo had done, but no, this town had a bit of the rough and tumble wild west left in it, and you could walk across the Stanton Street bridge over the Rio Grande into Mexico in fifteen minutes. Juarez had great museums, a Spanish language theater on the plaza, and an artist bar where painters gathered to talk about what is beautiful.

El Paso was great, but the university was the same old same old. Lots of backbiting among groups and plenty of down and dirty office politics. Why universities tend to be like this I do not fully comprehend. People have explained it using a proverb. Universities are made up of people who think themselves big fish but are forced to swim in a small pond. In the small pond there's a lot of energy and even intelligence but not much place for it to go. I've found that universities where professors are busy doing research and publishing are less that way. The faculty don't have much time for campus political games

Our apartment on Mesa Drive sat on a large and flat plateau between two deep arroyos that carried the rain off the Franklin Mountains down to the Rio Grande River. You always could tell where the river was south of our apartment by the green strip of irrigation along its banks. My sons would ruin pairs of pants playing with friends, sliding down the sides of the arroyos supposedly on flattened boxes. The apartment had a rule—no pets—but an old neighbor to my right, he was the exception that made the rule. John dressed always in rumpled shorts and a smudged t-shirt. He had a white stubble on his face and wore a Cubs baseball cap twisted to the side. John was from the Midwest like myself. I didn't see him much but when I did I'd stop to pet his cats and we'd talk about the Chicago Cubs, especially about the great player Ernie Banks. John lived alone and shyly kept to himself, but he truly loved cats. John was a feeder. He put out large mounds of dry food and milk for the wild cats who lived in the desert and arroyos—and they came up to get their nourishment brazenly both day and night.

My neighbor almost always had the door of his apartment open. Sometimes the cats went in; sometimes he would be at the door talking to them and feeding them. A slew of cats depended on him to survive. I assume they also hunted for mice, birds, and other creatures of the desert. When I'd stop to talk to John he was always kind. He was retired, trying to make do on social security. I never caught a strong odor coming out of his apartment so I gathered he did not let the cats in at night and kept them mostly outside. He had found a purpose in life. He had found love.

Eileen and I were not seeing much of each other in El Paso. The city is large and spread out because the Franklin Mountains pass through the middle. We spent a lot of time commuting in our blue Ford Pinto, taking the boys to their different schools on the west side of the city. She was teaching on one campus and I was teaching at another. One day I came out of the shower wrapped in a towel and something bit me on my big toe. The pain was worse than a wasp bite and I found myself leaping around the living room naked and on the left foot, trying to examine my toe, swearing a blue streak. When the pain settled down I went back into the hallway and started searching the shag carpet.

There he was. Mr. Scorpion. Not very big. This was the first scorpion I'd ever seen alive and up close. He looked as if he'd gotten hurt by our previous meeting. I had never imagined an in-house scorpion. Using a book I pushed him into a cereal bowl, then covered the bowl with the book. I went and opened the sliding glass door and tossed Mr. Scorpion over the back fence that surrounded our tiny patio. I began to wonder if cats in this part of the country could handle scorpions. Maybe I could get away with breaking the apartment regulations like John. Maybe I could tell the manager we needed a cat to protect our kids from scorpions.

I talked to my new El Paso friends, and some said that cats were immune to scorpion bites. I asked my neighbor John one evening after work, and his opinion was that the fur and thick skin of cats protected them.

"If you could tame one of my ferals, he'd keep you safe. Never had a scorpion in my place. These arroyo cats eat grasshoppers, lizards, scorpions—you name it. They're fast, good hunters and killers."

"You think I could tame a feral?" I asked.

"Nope. Maybe if a little one comes up."

"Do you think the apartment people would give me trouble?"

"Maybe. Maybe not. I told them my cats would keep the scorpions away. They got a lot of empty units here and they don't want the word getting out about the scorpions."

But I didn't get a cat. My wife Eileen and I split up. That story is a long one and doesn't need much mention here.

When I moved into the house of my second wife Courtney late in the year of 1975, she had a number of cats living with her at her small Gregory Street adobe house up the street from the Christian television station. Courtney, a writer like myself, was clearly a cat person and not a dog person. We'd been together about four months when she finished her MA in English and decided to go work on a PhD in creative writing at the University of Utah.

Courntey needed an income to support her three children and had a won a fellowship in creative writing. Her former husband had a bad drinking problem and had trouble keeping off the streets. When I met Courtney she was just coming off a number of years in an Evangelical Church where she had given up marijuana and booze. She was a flaming redhead with bright green Irish eyes who had lived an interesting and varied life. She'd run a typing business out of her home, been a race car driver, a seamstress, a legal assistant, a dinner theater actress, and for a short time in the mid-1960's, a bikini-clad woman who popped out of cakes at large all male executive gatherings. She called herself a "squatty body," but when she said that I thought she was being humble about her good looks.

Courtney was well read in a lot of American underground literature, from Henry Miller, to El Paso's John Rechy, to the beat writers, although when she entered Brother Matt's evangelical church, she burned her books and threw out her racing trophies. I couldn't however leave my job to follow Courtney north to the University of Utah. I had child support payments to make, so I remained in the far West Texas city of El Paso in Courtney's house with her cats and her eldest son Dusty while she used my pickup to drive up to Salt Lake City.

Dusty was a sophomore in high school and had taught himself to play great electric guitar in the back bedroom of the house, during his parent's divorce, as a means to deal with his pain. He was a lover of the excellent guitarist Joe Walsh. Dusty played Led Zeppelin's "Stairway to Heaven" so many times I wanted to plaster his guitar inside a wall. Dusty had what people used to call a "wandering eye" and now call dyslexia that surgeries had failed to correct and as a consequence he had difficulty reading. Dyslexia is viewed as a learning disability today. The bright florescents inside supermarkets and schools almost drove Dusty nuts. The longer Dusty was in school the less it interested him.

My first wife Eileen long felt she had never gotten what she wanted out of our relationship, and had even taken a course in assertiveness training to change our dynamics. After our marriage collapsed she soon found a new boyfriend and moved back to Austin, Texas, where we'd lived for two years while she got her MA in nursing. I had no notion this would happen when we divorced. Being separated from our two sons, even though I had not wanted children, was painful and hard because I had worked to be a good father.

My teenage stepson Dusty and I signed a contract on the behaviors we agreed on while he'd be living under my supervision and support. Later he admitted he had no intention of honoring the contract. He'd only signed it so he could stay in El Paso and hang with his buddies. After about a month I realized he was not regularly attending classes at El Paso High and was spending most of his time drinking with friends. I was surprised the high school never called me.

Summer vacation was not far away and I decided to rent the house out and send Dusty to his mother, who I hoped could handle him better than I. Courtney had this ability to engage in shouting matches with a teenage boy and yet remain calm and rational. I had no teen age children and had not yet mastered the skill.

But what to do with the cats?

I'd been sexually faithful to Courtney the many months she'd been gone, but I had not given up the company of others, both men and women, because when you live alone you especially need friends. I went out to dinner occasionally with groups of students, including ladies, and hung out sometimes at student apartments. With students I took short trips to see sights such as the state park Hueco Tanks east of El Paso where the Tigua Indians believe they first came into the world. I was young, and back in the 1970's spending time with students off campus was more common. Juarez, Mexico—just across the Rio Grande from El Paso—contained great restaurants and bars as well as a fantastic art museum whose domed ceiling was made from translucent stone. The architecture of the two cities and the mix of cultures made life edgy and exciting.

One student whose company I enjoyed was a black haired journalism major from El Paso Community College. Angela told me, quite oddly, that she didn't like me coming to her apartment because her roommate had larger breasts than she did. Some female competition was going on here, one not often revealed to men. I did get to go in once and meet her roommate and their Persian cat, who they called "Cat." They thought the name they'd given the cat was quite imaginative, and perhaps it was. Certainly it's a name you won't forget.

"Your cat seems a bit skinny," I told the roommate.

"We know," said Angela. "We think it's the breed."

"Does the cat throw up?" I asked.

"Not that we've seen," said Angela.

"Have you taken Cat to the vet?"

"Not yet," the roommate said. "We're students. We don't have money."

"I hear you," I said. "I've been there, many times, and I'm there now."

Courtney had my pickup, so Angela did the driving when we went to hang with other friends. A number of times, when she dropped me back at the house on Gregory, she offered to come in and have sex. There was a short period in the mid-seventies when women, under the spell of feminism, became more aggressive.

"Don't worry," she said. "I am not trying to break up your marriage. I'm horny."

She may have believed what she said, but I didn't. I told her I was leaving soon for the summer in Salt Lake City and wanted to rent the house, but needed to find a tenant who could tolerate and feed the yard cats. Angela told me she and her roommate were interested in the house. They needed a bigger place, and their current El Paso neighborhood didn't feel safe. A house that would tolerate their Persian would be perfect.

"I'm going to take an inexpensive small apartment when I get back at the end of the summer," I told Angela. "I don't need a large house."

Maybe I should have been suspicious. Perhaps I should have sensed that Jessica saw her offer to rent the house as a special favor she was doing for me, and that she hoped to see me move in with her when I got back at summer's end. I was a young college teacher and these were times when college teachers carried a flame of romantic allure.

I think some women believe college teachers made decent money and maybe they do, compared to some non-union Texas workers. Few realize how much work and stress is involved in college teaching. Few know the long three month "vacations" in the summer are actually three months unemployed and off salary, when a professor is still expected to do research and publish to advance in the job.

Up in Salt Lake City, later in the spring semester, Courtney seemed to have straightened out her teenage son by getting him enrolled in an alternative school. Poor Dusty, school had never been easy with his dyslexia. To keep from being bullied in school, he'd had to adopt a cool, tough macho front. The trouble is he lost in the process much of his original self, and the tough front didn't work well with those he was close to, like family and friends. It is a common male syndrome. You wall yourself off to survive, but then your own walls begin to strangle you.

I spent an enjoyable summer up in Salt Lake City in our second floor apartment in the Avenues. In August I started to prepare for the drive back to El Paso. I had the engine rebuilt in my grey Chevy pickup. Then a postcard arrived from Angela, accusing me of sticking her with the cats that ended up terrorizing her Persian. She then said she had turned these "wild cats" over to animal control and they'd been euthanized.

Three beautiful, wonderful cats belonging to Courtney—Sydney, Heaven, and Frog—cats that had been an important part of her life as she raised her children—were gone. Courtney became furious and weepy at the same time. She stayed home from summer work two days and wrote a long letter to Angela ordering her to move out of the house.

"I have the lease you signed right in front of me," she wrote, "and it specifically states you will feed the cats outside and allow them to remain on the property." She called in sick at her summer job and wrote Angela that we'd be down to El Paso in two days, a few weeks before her graduate classes started again. She was going to rent the place out to people she considered reliable.

"I helped Frog deliver her babies," she told me. "You don't know how many times Dusty risked life and limb climbing up on our tile roof to get Sidney down. Sidney was always climbing up the rose trellis on the side of the house, but never could figure out how to get down."

"I'm sorry," I said. "They seemed good people."

"I should have brought the cats with me," she said. "What do you know of taking care of a teenage boy or a batch of cats?"

She was right. My children were six and four and I'd never had much success with cats.

Chuck Taylor

9

A year later I had a cat of my own in Salt Lake City—a cat we called Percy that was given to me by a neighbor down the block who was high in the Mormon Church's education bureaucracy. He was the only African-American Mormon I'd ever met and had an interesting collection of small and medium sized meteorites in his back yard. Back in the late 1970's, the church had not yet changed its position that prevented African-Americans from entering the priesthood. I'd gotten fired from my teaching job in El Paso by running off with Courtney. I was now settled working as the Salt Lake City Poet-in-Residence under a government program called CETA. The new job involved less office politics and pleased me because I was working with seven other artists, including a dancer who ended up running off with the sculptor, and an Irish-American playwright whose Catholic grandfather had come to Utah to work in the mines.

Another neighbor across the street worked in the visitor center on the main temple grounds downtown where the Mormon Tabernacle Choir performs. Mathew had trained in the making of mechanical moving figures—animals and humans—at Disneyland in California. He told me as we sat together in the kitchen that the table where we drank ice water was the table he'd been born on. Mathew also informed me that when he did his missionary work in south Texas in the early-1960's, the Mexican-Americans he converted had turned whiter.

"Maybe with the fall season coming on," I suggested, "they were losing their summer tans."

One problem we faced is that Mormons nearly always had conversion in the backs of their minds. You were rarely an equal, but an inferior to be brought into the superior faith. It's a challenge to be friends with those who don't accept you for who you are. I could be talking with a Mormon acquaintance I hoped might become a friend, and then BOOM!–the conversion process would start. This was not true of all my Mormon friends and acquaintances, thankfully.

Suddenly in her second year of her PhD program, Courtney decided to return to Texas.

"Too much mind control," she said. "When the Mormon college kids write essays in my freshman classes, they say the same thing and use many of the same phrases and sentences."

She also said that strange men would follow her in cars as she walked from teaching at the University of Utah campus to our apartment in the avenues area, one of the first Mormon areas settled in Salt Lake City. I liked the neighborhood because we were one block from a woman's bookstore and an organic grocery.

To the east of the city stood the wonderful Wasatch Mountains. The downtown contained great bookstores, a live music club for gays and straights in an amazing cavernous warehouse, and two fine art-house movie theatres. A half block from our apartment was an old Mormon cemetery containing the grave of Joseph Smith II and his many wives.

We had lived in Salt Lake during the time Ted Bundy—the serial killer—escaped from prison, and during the time a leader of a polygamous fundamentalist group leaped to his death with his two wives and four children from a downtown hotel. Norman Mailer came to town researching his book, *Executioner's Song*, on another Utah serial killer, Gary Gilmore.

As a red-blooded Southerner, Courtney couldn't stand being in blue-uniformed, Yankee controlled, slave-free Utah. I told her that the Mormon leader Brigham Young during the civil war had contributed financially to both the northern and southern causes, but that did nothing to alter her point of view.

She left the cat Percy with me due to limited space in the pickup I'd lent her. She had to squeeze in most of her furniture and clothes and her three children. I was supposed to bring Percy to Texas when done with my CETA poet job. I didn't know what type of cat Percy was, but a friend of mine—more knowledgeable about breeds—claimed the cat was mostly a Cinnamon Angora. Its coat was long and silky. Sometimes I called Percy "Red Cat."

I liked Red Cat. The feline had a small edge of affection and maybe once a week would leap in my lap, or sleep on my bed in a far corner. Percy never stuck a cold nose in my face to wake me up at six am. She waited patiently by the bowl for me to feed her. The cat stayed mostly inside, but sometimes left the apartment by climbing out a back window onto a lower roof. The cat then leaped to the trunk of a black walnut and worked her way down.

I had no idea that Percy's condition had changed. Percy didn't look any different. I'm certain that Courtney was unaware of any problem when she fled back to Texas, or perhaps she was so anxious she too did not notice. I fed the cat twice a day. Maybe once a day I petted Percy, but beyond that I hardly looked the cat's way—unless on its own initiative the cat came my way. My attitude on cats at the time, based on previous experience, was that you were better off not pushing yourself on them unless the cat came looking for affection. Even today I think this practice works best with most cats.

To this day there's no way I can forget Percy coming into the bedroom in the pitch dark of three in the morning and letting out a bloody scream. During her long scream I recall doing what I thought then was a perfectly reasonable action. I reached down to the floor by the bed and grabbed one of my boots, and threw it in the direction

55

of the scream to get Percy to shut up and flee. A standard comedy bit in the movies when I was growing up was for people to throw shoes out windows at cats serenading the moon from the tops of fences.

I didn't open my eyes. I made no attempt to peer through the dark to take aim, so of course I missed Percy with the boot. In a moment my sleep-fogged brain cleared and I began to wonder if the scream had been made not to irritate but communicate an urgent need. I leaped out of bed and chased after Percy as the cat ran through the living room and turned into the kitchen and then took a sharp left down the hallway to the bathroom of our small apartment.

I followed Percy into the bathroom and caught a glimpse of a tail as the cat went inside the open door of the small linen closet at the end of the tub. I turned on the light and peered into the linen closet and noticed a small side hole at the floor made for a plumber to work on the tub's water pipes. This hole, amazingly, took you right inside the interior of the cast iron, porcelain-enameled bathtub. I loved that bathtub because it had legs and a high back, which meant the tub held the heat long and you could lay long in the water without having to drain and add more hot water.

"Oh Lord," I said next morning, tooth brush in hand, bent over near the linen closet. I heard some slight movement sounds.

Percy must have given birth to kittens inside the bathtub, way back at the far end, where it was impossible to reach them!

Percy was a SHE, and she had planned ahead and sought out before-hand the safest place to bear her babies. Her choice happened to be highly effective if a bit bizarre—inside an apartment's bathtub. I put food down as usual in the kitchen and expected Percy to bring forth soon her kittens from the tub. I took baths in the tub and at times tapped softly on the sides with a hammer, hoping to chase her and the babies out with the echoing noise.

After the month had passed, when it became time for me to

leave Utah and rejoin Courtney in Texas, I did the only thing I felt I could do.

Percy and her kittens had not emerged from her impenetrable fortress of the tub. I had failed in my many tricks to coax them out, so I packed up and left. Yes, I did an inappropriate thing. I abandoned a mother cat and her kittens. Of course I figured the landlord would discover the cats the next day when she came by to check out the place. Even if she took a few days, the mother and kitten had plenty of food and water.

I was going to try to drive back to Texas from Salt Lake City in a 1962 slant-six Plymouth Valiant lacking a back seat that I'd bought for thirty-five dollars from Joanie, a friend who'd come to Utah to study modern dance and worked at the woman's bookstore down the street. I kept the Valiant radiator from leaking by sticking fresh chewing gum in a tiny radiator hole every few days. If left unplugged a thin jet of hot water shot out like from a squirt gun, causing barelegged women crossing at intersections to do sensuous, sudden little dance steps, as if stung by a bee.

I had little funds left at my disposal because the CETA job paid poorly. The year was late in 1978. I had just enough to cover food and gas for the long drive back to Texas. With no money for a motel room, I ended up sleeping sitting up, in the packed Valiant, one night high in the cold Rocky Mountains of Colorado. If I'd called the landlord and explained the cat situation before I'd left, she might have demanded that I hire a plumber to get the mamma cat and kittens out. That would have required a longer stay in Salt Lake and money I lacked. When poor you have to make do, and making do means that sometimes you don't live up to middle class moral conventions. Looking back on my actions, living with a higher income, I am not exactly proud, but are those who are poor going to be forbidden to have pets? If not pets, why not forbid the poor to have children?

A week after I returned to El Paso, I got a disturbed letter from our former Salt Lake City landlord. She was not going to return our deposit, she explained, because she'd had to hire a plumber. He and his assistant were forced to remove the heavy tub, lug it down the narrow front stairs, and to stand it in the front yard to gently shake out the mother cat "Percy" and her kittens.

Did they really need to take the whole tub down the stairs? Maybe the landlord had made that part up.

I knew that, given time, the mother and kittens, out of curiosity, would emerge on their own. I had left plenty of provisions behind on the kitchen floor.

A few weeks after I returned, we finished visiting in El Paso. The post-Angela renters were doing a fine job with the house. We started driving the long journey to east Texas, to live in the town of Edgewood where Court-ney's paternal grandparents had spent their lives as sharecroppers. I drove my pickup, and Courtney drove the slant-six Valiant, which amazingly was still running. Courtney had spent many summers in Edgewood with her grandma and grandpa and she said she loved the place. The town was close to Lake Towakoni and not far from the piney woods of east Texas.

Fifty miles east of Dallas, we knew we'd crossed an imaginary line into the true South when we first saw three men "hunkered down" on a front lawn in Wills Point talking to one another. I hadn't seen men talking this way since living in North Carolina as a child. We stopped for coffee and then briefly stepped into a corner boot maker's shop that her grandfather had told her was world famous. Six miles east from Wills Point was our destination—Edgewood—a town that managed fine with one traffic light.

10

By September of 1978 Courtney and I were comfortably resettled in an old house in Edgewood. As something of a welcoming gift, one of our neighbors gave us a cat. Our house was a rambling old three-bedroom structure with a large front porch and a half-acre side yard. We had plenty of room for a cat. The creature was a little black, brown and white kitty that did not gambol-play like your typical kitty. Arnold did not get up inside the box spring by ripping a hole in the thin cotton cover underneath, and he did not get inside a paper bag and scramble around to everyone's delight. Arnold, we learned, lay mostly on his side sleeping, never curled up neatly in usual kitten fashion.

We were financially stressed, null and void on the cash flow, especially with Christmas upon us. Both of our vehicles broke down shortly after we moved in, and we did not have the money to take the cat to the veterinarians ten miles south in Canton. We decided we did not want to risk getting worm eggs in the carpet and then in our stomachs, so we banished the poor cat to the front porch.

The cat would sleep right by the front screen door, and if you opened the door and did not block the kitten with your foot, he'd somehow gather the energy to dash inside and you'd have to carry him out again and then go scrub your hands. Here was an animal, different from many cats, who wanted to be an inside cat.

We kept a small bowl of water close by the door for Arnold as well and a clear plastic Tupperware container of cat food. The poor fellow—he seemed so hungry for affection and companionship.

I felt terrible. I know Courtney and her three kids felt the same.

Finally I put Arnold in a cardboard box and walked three miles west along the railroad tracks to the town dump. Edgewood was made up of about a thousand people, located sixty miles east of Dallas on Highway 80. I was trying to write poetry and stories; Courtney was working on a folklore book. We ate a lot of fresh yard eggs that year from our chicken coop, and plenty of vegetables from our garden.

I was always dreaming I would spend a week knocking on everyone's doors, shaking hands and introducing myself. With just a thousand people in Edgewood, it seemed possible I might get to know every one and then acquire a broader and deeper understanding of human nature. Who knows? Maybe someone would have taken Arnold.

I did spend one day going from door to door, trying to register people to vote. I got discouraged when I met a man who had killed a bobcat in the creek behind his house—the only bobcat he'd ever seen. He kept it stuffed on top of the television.

After about a thirty minute walk I reached the dump on the far west side of town close to the railroad track, beyond the saw mill and cemetery. A retarded young man worked there along with the dump supervisor. The supervisor referred to the skinny young man as "not all there." I liked that expression because it suggested a full humanity, that part of this blond-haired young man was perhaps up with God in heaven.

When I reached the dump I noticed a long deep trench recently dug in the red earth as a new place to bury the town's trash. The supervisor was off for lunch.

"Do you have a dump cat?" I asked the retarded man. "How about a cat to keep the mouse and rat population down?" Back then no one knew the politically correct euphemisms such as "special needs."

When the young man saw Arnold he got excited, the same way we all get excited when we see a young cat. I gave the blond man the box and cat. Maybe here this poor cat would find both a home and love.

I remember the young man wore a plaid flannel shirt and a dusty blue cap. I told him not to play with the cat too much. I explained that I'd never seen a cat in this condition before and didn't know what the animal's problem was. No vet had done an examination.

"It's possible the cat's ill," I said. "I wouldn't touch him too much."

"We're tough," the young man said.

I saw the young man from the dump about a month later down at the grocery store in Edgewood's small downtown area. He told me he lived in a shack a mile out of town along HW 80 that a farmer had given him. That struck me as a better solution than sticking the man in the large state institution nearby, Terrill State Mental Hospital. Since his shack was in the direction of my house, we both hiked east together along the railroad tracks. He told me that many people in Edgewood refused to speak to him.

The young man said that Arnold liked to be with him in the small hut at the front of the dump, and that he was trying now to catch mice.

"Any luck?" I asked.

"Nope," the man said. "But he'll catch a cricket now and then."

I considered inviting the man in for coffee, since we were not far from my house, but figured he needed to get his groceries home to the refrigerator. Today, this man might be diagnosed as autistic, or perhaps with Asperger syndrome. Neither conditions make a person social—at least usually.

Chuck Taylor

11

A few months later we'd acquired another cat from a different neighbor. Little did we know that our new cat Rosy was pregnant. Courtney and I needed to take off for a two-week job in Victoria, Texas, to work as artists-in-the-schools. We were close to down to our last dimes and desperately needed the work to support not only ourselves but Courtney's three kids. Courtney at first had continued to study and read for her PhD in creative writing from the University of Utah, but one day threw one of the novels from her comprehensive exam list across the room and declared herself done with getting degrees. We could not count on any money coming in from graduate fellowships she might receive to supplement the part-time teaching job I'd taken at the University of Texas at Tyler.

Courtney decided she was going to be "famous in Texas," a best selling writer in her home state. That was enough for her.

"You can't live on the income from your fame or on book sales in one state," I argued, although I was going on a what I thought was a realistic hunch and had no facts to back me up.

Out back of our Edgewood home, in the corner of the lot by the fence, was our home-built chicken coop with a leopard painting on it. Courtney had gotten inspired one day in Salt Lake City to paint the leopard, when the chicken coop was an enclosed area on the back of my pick up. Since the rooster fertilized all the eggs, we decided to save a batch from the cast iron skillet and hatch more hens to lay more eggs. More eggs meant we could cut our grocery bill even more. I built a wooden box, put dried grass in the bottom and a grill from the refrigerator on top. I put two bricks on top to keep the grill solidly in-place, along with a gooseneck lamp with its light on and pointed down to keep the eggs warm.

In the morning Courtney, her three kids, and I scrunched into the front seat of my old grey pickup that I'd gotten working again and set off on the long drive south and east of San Antonio to Victoria. The Valiant had finally kicked the bucket, thrown a rod, on a jaunt into Dallas to visit the old art museum in art deco designed Fair Park. We arrived in Victoria late in the afternoon. We found the apartment the Art's Council had arranged for us in a pleasant neighborhood close to the Victoria Zoo in an neighborhood full of mansions.

Suddenly I remembered pregnant Rosy back in Edgewood. I remembered an obscure way to get inside the house through the hole in the floor where an old water heater used to be. The water heater once sat in a tiny closet in the kitchen. The closet door did not lock and a cat could figure out how to paw it open. Rosy was supposed to be staying with the lady who gave her to us while we were gone, but a cat is always curious. A cat will explore and wander looking for a safe place to be or for food. Rosy probably wondered where we had gone, and was searching for a hideaway to have her babies.

Don't worry, I told myself. Rosy can't get the grill off the top of the wooden box after the chicks hatch, what with the bricks there. I'd left plenty of food and water in the box for the chicks. The cat might be smart enough to push the lamp off. She might, as a result, set the house on fire, but she wouldn't be strong enough to slide the bricks off the grate.

When we returned to the house two weeks later, I was not happy with what I discovered. Fortunately, when the cat knocked the lamp off the wood box containing the chicks, the hot light bulb had shattered. The chicks, however, were nowhere to be found. What we did find were chick feathers all over the living room carpet.

Why didn't Rosy get a chicken bone caught in her throat? Because cats have always eaten birds with hollow bones and are careful. When we got back, Rosy was gone and we did not see her until after her kittens were raised and on their own. Perhaps her kittens had needed the extra protein from the baby chicks, and other animals had eaten the dried cat food we'd left on the porch.

Perhaps she felt she'd done a bad thing and was worried about our response. I doubt it though. She was merely following her natural instinct to hunt. Those of us who buy our meat wrapped in plastic at the supermarket—are we better than Rosy, or do we hire a butcher to do the killing for us? All our hens in the chicken coop remained undisturbed. We'd hired the boy from across the street to feed them and gather their eggs to take home for his mother to cook.

In Edgewood a cat lady lived a few houses down from out house toward the railroad tracks. Like many small towns, the old downtown along the tracks suffered. The coming of the automobile meant that most of the successful retail trade had relocated south to the main highway. We walked by the cat lady's house every day on our way to get the mail at the small post office downtown. Edgewood was too small for door-to-door delivery.

The cat lady's house was a modest place, a two bedroom built of brick in the suburban ranch style of the mid 1950's. In the years we knew her from 1978 to 1996, she lost three husbands, but she continued to keep cats. I couldn't go inside her house because the smell was overwhelming. Her neighbor on the other side, the town auto mechanic Dusty, tried to help her out with minor house repairs because she was elderly. Dusty could get inside the house but claimed he had to get out every fifteen minutes. Otherwise he'd grow dizzy and pass out.

In October of the first year we lived in the town, in 1978, one of the cat woman's sons had been visiting during a week of constant heavy rain, and when my pickup got stuck in the drainage ditch that ran along the street, he helped me dig the vehicle out, rounding up a bunch of rocks from his mother's back yard that we stuck under my jack. I was always chasing the cat lady's cats out from under our house by banging pans or tossing sticks. I often thought of calling the county sheriff about the health hazard for the whole neighborhood. I never did call because her son had stayed with me alongside the road in the miserable mud and pouring rain, both of us soaked to the skin, until we got my pickup's back tire out of a rut that had it down to the back axle.

In small towns systems of obligation develop. As an outsider Yankee, I much appreciated that Edgewood's small gestures included me. This small east Texas town was not as shut off from strangers as one might expect. It was an atypical town. Later they elected a black mayor, had a black police chief named Joe Willy, and the town had integrated its schools right after the US Supreme Court's decision, with no passive resistant schemes to get around the new law of the land, unlike Grand Saline ten miles east. In the 1940's Grand Saline had race riots; in the 1970's no blacks lived there. Edgewood was a poor man's town, made up mostly of small houses, people said, that'd belonged to agricultural workers and share croppers who traveled out to work the fields..

The cat lady's second husband loved to ride a power lawnmower. He was more agile on the mower than he was on his feet. His balance wasn't so great and he drove the mower like a drunkard, but he loved it so much that many times he cut my yard for the fun of it. While on the mower he'd chase his wife's cats. He'd even chase our ducks, laughing and laughing above the roar of the engine. It was all for sport, and he never hurt a single animal.

With his fast-moving rider mower he could do our yard in twenty minutes. With my small hand pushed machine it took an hour, so that was another reason I never complained about the cat lady's menagerie of cats. How all her husbands managed to adapt to the smell I never found out. What else but love? She was a woman in her mid-fifties when we first met, an overweight countrywoman, and not what you'd call movie star attractive in her old cotton print dresses. She may have been a good Southern cook and been good in bed. Of course, none of the old men were Hollywood hunks either.

Our large white house on the eastern edge of Edgewood was supposed to be a stepping stone to a small place in the country, a small farm of say thirty acres where we could grow our own food organically and commute into a larger town like Tyler for part-time work, but Courtney had found out she was a city gal and couldn't stand living in small towns and being around her conservative small town Texas aunts and uncles.

Her change of attitude broke my heart. We all have dreams, but how many of us ever get to live our dreams? In October of 1979 we gave away our goats, our chickens, our ducks, and our cats to Courtney's biker brother Sam who had ten acres outside of Oklahoma City. A Vietnam vet, he lived on disability from the military and worked part-time as a truck driver. Sam kindly drove down from Oklahoma City to Edgewood to fetch all our creatures. It hurt to see him carry them off, but with Sam we hoped the animals would be happy in the larger space of his ten acres.

We kept only Minky dog, and then packed up and moved the family to a neighborhood in East Dallas. In less than two years we lived in two apartments on the poor end of Swiss Avenue. Courtney and I spent many months working for Kelly Services all over the city of Dallas. The experience gave us an amazing picture of the diversity of work in this country. A year later in 1980 we packed up again and moved south to Austin with the utopian notion of buying a city communal house with my former wife Eileen. The only way we could see ourselves affording Austin was to put three adults and five kids under one big roof. It might have actually have ended up being four adults and seven children, because Eileen's housemate Enrique wanted in on the deal also.

Of course, that idea didn't pan out. Enrique, we learned, was totally broke and could not squeeze a dime out of his wealthy Mexican father. He couldn't contribute a nickle toward the down payment. Also, I recalled that the Chinese character for TROUBLE was drawn as something like two women under the same roof, sharing the same kitchen. We ended up, Courtney and I and her kids, sleeping in a downtown dusty bookstore basement and operating a used bookstore. I can still recall potential customers calling and asking Courtney over the phone, "Do you sell adult books?"

And she replying, "Why, yes, most of our books are for adults, but we also have a children's section."

I loved working in the bookstore. Carrying books around and putting them on selves was great exercise. At the counter I felt like a bartender for those addicted to the drink of words. I served up delicious books stirred with friendship and a compassionate ear. Readers are a special brand of people, and in the eight years we operated the store, we suffered only two bounced checks.

12

In 1986 I'd gotten a box of three small kittens from my mechanic friend Dusty up the road. Since I was living by myself back in Edgewood, replacing the roof on the house we still owned, and commuting over to Dallas on the weekends to work in a used bookstore, I had time to give to the kittens and greatly appreciated their cuddly company.

Dusty had taken me out to see the kittens in the large metal mechanics shop he'd built behind his house. Dusty was a short, powerfully built man, and not only repaired automobiles but played drums in a rock and roll band. He was in the process of relocating his auto repair business down the road to larger digs, and the old shop was now unlighted, moodily quiet and dark inside. Sometimes the wind shook the aluminum siding. Dusty picked up a stick and led me to the box where three kittens were kept.

Dusty leaned over the box, stretched out an arm to pick up a kitten, and then suddenly leaped back and let out a "Whoa!" Since I was standing next to him I leaped back too. My heart did a rapid skip-jump.

"Did you see that?" he asked.

"See what?" I replied.

"You know sometimes around here a snake will kill a cat," he added. "The mate will know, and the mate will find and catch that snake to bring it back for its kittens to kill and eat as revenge."

"Sure, Dusty, sure. You've laid these stories on me before. Remember the alligator tortoise that bit your toe when you were fishing in the Sabine River? You had to wait until dusk when he came up for air before you could get free and out of the water?"

"You don't believe me?"

Dusty took the stick he was carrying and stuck it into the box where the kittens slept. He lifted the stick up and hanging on it was what looked like a black, greasy piece of rope—or a dead snake. It was hard to tell in the old shop's shadows.

I stepped back farther. I could see him teasing me, threatening to chase me around the shop with whatever the thing was hanging from the stick.

"Come look," Dusty said. He pointed the stick down and the object slid onto the cement floor. Whatever was on the floor did not move.

I came up and was surprised to see it was indeed a dead snake.

"You put it there," I said. "You planned all along to trick me. You gave yourself away when you picked up the stick when we first walked in here."

"Nah, I didn't put the snake there," Dusty laughed, dodging my accusation. "Mother cats will kill snakes and bring them back for their babies to eat."

"Those babies are cute," I said after I'd taken a close look and held them. "Why don't you want them around?"

"I've, like, ten cats already, thanks to the cat lady next door."

"OK. All right. I'll take them."

Courtney, about a week later, decided to ride the bus up from Austin to Edgewood for a visit. The first day she was in town, Courtney meandered into the front empty bedroom where her daughter Faith had slept when small and I'd told Faith bedtime stories of Snapper, the super grasshopper with X-ray vision, and of Snarfy, the train-riding circus cat who protected big elephants from tiny evil mice. Ah Faith, she was a good looking blond now, a high school dropout who saw herself as grown up and made her living selling flowers on Sixth Street to the lonely strollers and rock and rollers till the wee hours of the morning. Dear Faith, she took such joy in living and was in a rush to get on with the all of her life.

I was in the process, there in Edgewood, of scraping off the hard oil paint someone long ago had put over the lovely small windows in the bedroom door. Courtney went to the small closet to take a short, loving look at the three new kittens I'd adopted.

I'd been up in East Texas for about three months, doing repairs on the house where Courtney and I had lived and written books in back in the late 1970's. Since that time it had at times sat empty but mostly been rented out to a nurse who commuted to Terrill State Mental Hospital, a place I had once worked at for a short while with drugged patients the state hoped I could get back into society by teaching them money management.

Courtney had come to visit and to check how the repair work was progressing. She then stayed with me, doing her share of work for a productive three months, but finally returned to Austin, lonesome for her grown children, sick of conservative East Texas, and impatient with how long the repairs were taking. Still I was glad for the company and appreciated her help with the work.

Courtney, a few days after her arrival, picked up one of the kittens to cradle in her arms. The kitty lay still for a moment. Courtney was smiling, and then, all of a sudden, the kitten kicked, leaped, fell, and landed on the wooden bedroom floor. The baby jerked a moment and then was still.

Courtney looked in my eyes. Her heart had cracked; she was suddenly so vulnerable and unsure. It was a face on her I hadn't seen in a while. I'd been working two days a week fifty miles away in Dallas. When home I'd worked hard on the roof, removing three layers of shingles, re-decking one side, and putting on new shingles, yet Courtney seemed unappreciative. She remained distant, complaining on how long the work was taking, even though she lived off of my meager salary and was unable to help pay for any repair supplies.

For a moment I wanted to leave her in pain, to get her back for the almost hourly sharp remarks that had begun since she arrived in Edgewood. She seemed out to blame me for all our economic woes, and did not take any responsibility herself. This I found odd in a woman who valued independence and espoused so many feminist beliefs in person and in writing. But then I remembered when the same kitten disaster had happened to me at the hospital when I was four. I went forward and put my arms around Courtney and assured her what had happened could happen to anyone.

13

Before I returned to Austin after finishing the repairs on the house, I took the two remaining cats cats, now grown, over to the veterinarian in Canton for possible adoption. I had to beg a ride from a neighbor who owed me a favor because my Oldsmobile had quit on me from all the work commutes to Dallas. I lacked the funds to fix it and planned to ride the Greyhound to Dallas and then down to Austin. I'd always loved bus rides for the oppor-tunity to visit with people.

I'd become friends with the only Mexican-American living in Edgewood that I knew of. Armando was retired from the Santa Fe railroad that passed through town, and owned an entire city block. He had turned his block into an incredible Garden of Eden, and every year I bought a case of raw honey from his hives to give to friends as a Christmas present. Armando gave me a ride to the vet in Canton, who at first refused to take the young cats. The vet only relented when I made my threat, "Well, I guess I'll carry them out into some nearby woods in a box and let them go." The whole country had no animal shelter.

I felt bad about doing this, but Courtney was back living in a small, inexpensive apartment in East Austin on Manor Road, and the lease stipulated no cats. The landlord Marcus lived in an apartment down below, so I doubted we could get away with sneaking cats in. He owned other apartments in California and spent about half the month in Austin. The landlord employed his own seventy year old father as a maintenance man in the building.

I suppose I've inherited much of my Depression era parents' attitudes toward pets: that you were doing your loving duty if you feed and water them and keep them out of extreme cold. We were poor, struggling writers, Courtney and I, at this point in our lives, and being connected to the Depression through our parents made how we lived easier to handle. I shudder to think what will happen to those generations after us if the rough times we are experiencing continue for long or get worse. Many cannot imagine life without Blue Ray high definition television, air conditioning, iPods, video games, and computers. I enjoyed a marvelous life a long time without these technological marvels. I recall cutting wood and putting the kindling in my grandmother's wood stove. Guess what? I was as happy then as I am now.

My feelings about cats had become confused, because of my unlucky experiences with them. I yearned to care for a cat but seemed cursed, fated to live in a bad dream. I can't complain too much because overall my life had been a good one, blessed by good passions, great adventures, good friends, and plenty of people to love. My childhood experience with our family cat running away, slipping out a cracked car window, suggested to me cats were better than dogs at surviving on their own, and not particularly dependent on people. We have a friend Kazumi who sometimes leaves her small white lapdog at our house while running errands. The dog tries to climb in her lap while she drives. Kazumi has left the little one with us many times. Still, each time the dog will shiver, whimper, search around the house, and stare out the window, never resting until her owner returns.

Has anyone known a cat to behave that way?

My friend Jadene, the poet, takes care of a bitter cat. Bitter cat spends most of her time on a bed in a back room where Jadene's son Mick sleeps when he visits. The cat is bad tempered because her original owner, Mick, had to turn his cat over to his mother because his new dog tried to kill it. Whenever Mick comes from Austin to visit his mother and father in Bryan the cat is overjoyed. This suggests that a few cats do indeed get attached to specific humans.

The way veterinarians fuss over animals these days, with the demand that animals come in for yearly physicals and get all sorts of shots not required by the county, strikes me, as a child raised by depression parents, as an improper attempt to turn pets into humans, and as an improper attempt by veterinarians to take advantage of people's feelings and make themselves wealthy. When the golden retriever I raised from a puppy developed cancer, the veterinarian wished to cut him open from top to bottom to remove the tumors, and then have him go through chemotherapy and radiation. With a human, you can explain why you are taking such extreme measures. I could not put my dog through such suffering— treatments that had less than 30% chance of success—because he would not know why. I just couldn't do it to him. He'd already suffered through some pretty rough treatments, and it seemed his gentle eyes were always wondering why. I have known humans who have turned down extreme treatments, some because of the pain, some because they lacked health insurance.

But, as I said, I was leaving the house in Edgewood to return to my family in Austin. Courtney's small apartment in Austin was located in a unique clothing optional facility, and many residents lounged around the swimming pool or walked around the inside courtyards in their birthday suits. The place was designed so that no one from the outside could see in. Many residents played volley ball in the nude; some even gardened in the courtyard garden patch in the buff. After a while, the nudity began to seem commonplace and I forgot about it. Because many of the residents truly believed that nudism removed class barriers enforced by the style of clothes people wore, New Manor Apartments functioned like a village and one had the pleasure of getting to know all sorts of types—some quite idealistic.

A few months into my life at New Manor, I invited a poet/professor friend, his wife, and teenage daughter over for dinner. The shocked, buffaloed look on their faces, when a woman and man walked by our open door holding hands in the total buff, will remain humorously burned in my memory forever. Somehow all three of my visitors had come through the locked doors and missed the large posted signs that read, "THIS IS A CLOTHING OPTIONAL FACILITY." I had not informed them beforehand because I didn't want to make a big deal out of the nudity, and because I was concerned, even though they were old friends, that they might turn judgmental and refuse to come.

I had not been highly motivated to keep the nearly grown Edgewood kittens because, though affectionate, they had given me what turned out to be a serious case of ringworm. I had long streaks of red across my stomach, back, and chest, as well as the characteristic ringworm circles on the backs of my arms. Looking as I did, I wasn't going to be working up a great tan going nude, chillin' out with the beautiful people around the courtyard swimming pool.

Courtney told me first that what I had gotten might be ringworm, but it was not from the cats.

"Have you ever *seen* ringworm?" I asked.

"No," she admitted, "but I've had plenty of cats."

"These cats I got from Dusty. He kept them out in the old shop behind his house with a dead snake in their bed. What can you expect?"

"Maybe it's not ring worm," Courtney said. "I bet you got a rash from your lousy bathing habits."

"Well thanks a lot," I said. "It took twelve years of marriage to judge my bathing habits?"

"I didn't want to hurt your feelings," she said.

"There are good ways to deliver a harsh message," I came back.

I went to the People's Clinic in the basement of the Congregational Church on the vendor's market street across from the University of Texas. It was the cheapest place I knew to get medical treatment. I'd done volunteer work there a few years back and knew most of the staff. My first wife Eileen and her husband had worked there for years. Austin hippies and political radicals in the sixties had started the clinic, and back in more utopian times every worker made the same wage, whether doctor or janitor.

The young doctor, who looked to me like he still belonged in high school, took a quick glance at my arm and chest and confirmed I had ringworm. He was a new doctor that I did not know.

"Have you been around a lot of cats lately?" he asked.

"Yeah," I said. "Smothered in cats, you might say."

"All cats carry ringworm, but some have it worse than others," the doctor said. "Some people are most sensitive to ringworm than other people."

He sat at his small desk, doodling with a pencil on a prescription pad. My case was clearly not that interesting. "Were these cats you were smothered in city cats or country cats?"

"The latter."

"I'm going to give you this topical cream to apply. It should clear the ringworm up in a few weeks."

I spread the white lotion all over the red areas for three weeks. I went out on the balcony of our apartment, as advised by the doctor, to give my infected skin short sun treatments. The red areas did not respond to the cream or the sun and continued to grow larger. I pictured my entire body covered with the red rash of ringworm in another month. The itching was severe but I fought the urge to scratch because I knew it would make the rash worse.

I went again to the doctor at People's Clinic.

"Not working, eh?" He said. "I do have a pill you can take, but it has not been on the market long. There's liver damage reported in a percentage of patients."

"Oh, great," I said. "I already had liver trouble. I had hepatitis B back in 1977."

"Have you had a liver function test?"

"A couple of times. I tested out fine. I used to say I got the Hep from drinking the water across the border in Juarez, Mexico, when I lived in El Paso. El Paso's sewer system and treatment plant, I'd been told, was on higher land than Juarez's water treatment plant, and that made for contamination by underground seepage. The explanation made my Mexican-American friends angry. They considered it insulting, so I stopped using it."

"Well... do you want to wait and try the cream a couple more weeks?"

"No," I countered. "I've always had sensitive skin. Get me within a quarter mile of poison oak or ivy and I break out all over."

I took home the pills and took three each day after meals. Within a week the itchy red rash had cleared up. I was so relieved. The poison ivy I'd caught at Camp Pinnacle the summer between forth and fifth grades had covered my entire face and chest, condemning me to isolation in a small cabin for weeks. I worried then I'd be permanently disfigured. Whenever I get ill I remember my years as a small child with asthma, lying in bed for days at a time, wondering if I will be able to pull enough air into my lungs to survive through another night to the next day.

"If you'd been cleaner, you wouldn't have gotten into trouble," Courtney announced again.

"All sorts of people get ringworm," I responded. "It's common with cats. Do you even know what ringworm is?"

"Sure. A small parasite worm."

"Sorry, but you're wrong. It's a fungus, my dear, a microscopic plant, and no soap you bathe in will kill it since ringworm roots down into the muscle below the skin. I hope you know hamburger isn't ham."

Courtney went back to reading her book. She looked a bit embarrassed. She was tense, working without wages at our old bookstore, which was struggling to pay the rent and sales tax. She had promised more than once to find a paying job but had not kept that promise. The funds we lived on came from my UT teaching job.

Shortly after I had ringworm, my close friend Mike, who worked at Seton hospital, told me the story of a parasite that had gotten into the litter box of a cat. The parasite had transferred to the cat owner while he was washing out the plastic litter box. Once inside the owner the parasite had attacked the man's nervous system and he'd died.

"If you have a cat," my ultrasound tech friend Mike said, "you don't want to keep a litter box inside. Make sure it's clay litter and that you change the litter every few days."

Since then I have never touched a litter box, and I try to live in places where there are no litter boxes and where the cats can go outside and do their business.

We assume, since cats and humans have lived together some six thousand years, we are immune to each other's illnesses. Lately however there's been some research suggesting that humans can get toxoplasmosis from cats and that the disease can cause neurologic problems. So far the weight of evidence suggests such problems will occur only in people with weakened immune systems. Despite my generally unlucky life with cats, I plan to cut cats a break unless further research becomes conclusive.

I still believe the universe will provide one cat I'm meant for, and one cat that's meant for me. It's called hope. Hope is built into our bones and keeps us going.

Chuck Taylor

14

I must not forget Skitzy, the cat this tale is dedicated to, the cat Courtney and I first acquired on the 225-acre Dobie Ranch in the Texas hill country south of Austin in 1986. We went to the Dobie when Courtney won a writer's fellowship that paid her bills and let her write for six months with supposedly no worries. Actually, however, both of us ended up worrying all the time. We worried about how we would feed and house ourselves after we left, since we both had given our bookstore jobs to others and I no longer worked for the University of Texas. Courtney also fretted over her grown children, who were going through big adolescent troubles back in Austin, not the best place perhaps for adolescent troubles.

Although we appreciated the opportunity to be out at the Dobie Ranch, with Barton Creek flowing through the property and the lovely remote Texas hill country all around us, we left with sighs of relief. We'd come up with a good scheme to continue writing and living in the hill country, but closer to the center of Austin and to Courtney's kids. Our cat Skitzy moved with us to the mesquite and cedar woods on a limestone ridge about a mile from Barton Creek Mall. The new location would not be much different than the territory the cat was familiar with on the ranch. We all know how poorly cats take to changes of location.

At the Dobie in the hill country, Skitzy often brought snakes and lizards she'd killed to the back door as gifts. At sunrise Courtney and I would spot in the dissipating fog four or five deer grazing in the front yard. In a moment, they would appear to walk through the five-foot fence around the yard and disappear down the rocky hill toward the creek.

Courtney and I had both grown fond of the young cat. How the feline came to be ours I can't say for sure. I recall vaguely she was a gift from the balloon clown Mary, who needed to leave her house for an apartment, due to a cutback in her hours at the Balloon Boutique. Our goal after we left the Dobie Ranch was to spend six more months rent-free in tents in the woods across from Austin's Barton Creek mall in order to continue writing, but Courtney soon grew tired of the solitude of the campsite and of the leaky tents we'd pitched above Barton Creek. Despite her promises, she abandoned Skitzy and me for the allure of the city and to be closer to her grown children. Austin usually has warm winters, yet how many folks can handle staying in tent, camping out in the woods, and cooking over an open fire in January?

Skitzy, my dog Minkie, and I would take long hikes together along Barton Creek, enjoying the waterfalls and the cliffs rising on both sides of the crystal clear spring water. Skitzy, unlike my dog, was not interested in sniffing around. She enjoyed being with us, her small tribe, and she enjoyed doing a little hunting. We were located in woods where we rarely saw other people, and the young cat would hike miles and miles with us through twists and turns along the spring fed creek, farther and farther away from the city. Little though she was, she was not afraid and, though small, not at all weak.

Skitzy would dash ahead (but always within eye distance), stop, crouch in the grass and wait, and then she'd dash ahead again. One day we three were walking up a slight incline toward our camp. Suddenly she leaped almost straight up in the air and caught a bird mid-flight. I hadn't seen the bird. Skitzy dropped to the ground, her teeth on the small bird's neck, and then put her paw on its back to break it's spine. I hated to see the bird killed yet I admired Skitzy's hunting skills. When you live in the wild you must expect wildness.

Since leaving the woods Courtney and I had not been seeing eye to eye on many issues. She was threatening, "to split the blanket" if I continued to stay in the woods. She made it clear: the choice was either the woods or her. I must give up my Thoreauvian life and the book I was writing about the experience—or she'd leave me. I'd never practiced such brinkmanship in a relationship and I didn't know whether to take her seriously or to see if she'd back down. I knew if I said I was going to leave someone, I wouldn't be bluffing. Leaving is not to be bluffed. I'd leave, period—no games, no vacillation.

"I don't think Skitzy will be able to survive in the city, " I told Courtney. "She's happy here. She's a forest cat."

"It's either the woods or me," my wife repeated. "You don't want to be out there when a blue norther' blows in."

"The real cold's a ways away, and Texas winters can be mild. I've time to prepare. It's the rain I'm working on getting prepared for now. You should see how I've fixed the tents so they are covered with tarps and can't leak. I've dug trenches so the groundwater runs away from the tents. You should see the winter garden I've planted."

Courtney was unmoved. There's no way she'd go back to the woods, yet I decided to call what I sensed to be a bluff. I'd made a promise to myself to live like the famous Henry David Thoreau in the woods and write about it. I was going to stick with the project a while longer.

When the six months were over, I packed up my elaborate campsite with its three tents and moved back to Austin. My friend Mike was a big help transporting my gear, since the giant, gas-guzzling, politically incorrect 1978 Oldsmobile station wagon I owned was not running. I also moved Skitzy cat and Minkie dog with me into downtown Austin where we stayed in the basement of a used bookstore, Books and More, that we'd started six years earlier.

The store was a dilapidated but grand place, located in an old warehouse building on a north-south street in Austin's downtown. In the main room the various workers organized and sponsored plays, poetry readings, art shows, and for a while, an original songwriter's circle produced by an Austin singer/songwriter who'd once been my student. All this went on, despite the fact that every quarter the store struggled to make its sales tax payments.

Minkie dog had lived in the bookstore before. If I was not around, she was smart enough, as a border collie, to walk herself out the door and find a patch of grass a short distance away to take care of business. The dog even knew how to navigate across busy streets safely on her own. Minkie didn't like the basement and greatly missed the woods, as any dog would, but she could deal with the place.

The border collie had walked up to my stepdaughter and me one summer day back in 1979 as we crossed the railroad tracks in Edgewood. The dog had adopted us, chosen us to be her care givers. Minkie's the name my stepdaughter Faith chose for her. Minkie never required a leash because she never ran off. When we took her for a walk she always paced about ten feet in front of us, and she always came when I whistled. The dog barked only if there was a serious intruder on our "space"—not when people were walking by—and she never begged at the table.

Without any training whatsoever, she was the smartest and most perfectly behaved dog I'd ever known. I'd had other dogs that were at times trials. No need to go off much into that, beyond mentioning that I disliked one dog so much I named him "Checkers" after President Nixon's dog. The creature must have disliked our family as much as I disliked Nixon, for Checkers always was trying to run away. One late afternoon, after I'd spent an two hours chasing him down to bring him home, he looked at me, I looked at him, and we connected. I opened the car door and let him go. Yes, I've had trouble with dogs as I've had trouble with cats. If you respect a pet, you're called to respect the animal's major choices. This dog wished to be free and we lived where there was plenty of open territory. Who can blame him? I lived in early 1975 on the edge of Austin, along the Colorado River in married student housing. Perhaps the dog would find a ranch to be happy on.

The cat Skitzy however was another matter. She was a country cat and had never been in the city. We had given her the name Skitzy because she was a nervous cat and spooked easily. Sure enough, when we got settled into the windowless cement basement of the bookstore, Skitzy could not adjust to the bad air and dim gloom—or to the noise and traffic upstairs outside the door on downtown Austin streets. I would take her walking mornings and afternoons in Republic Square, a small park a block away. One day she slipped her collar off and dashed across the street between passing cars and slipped up an alley.

I spent the rest of that morning and all afternoon, until dark, looking for Skitzy. I looked the whole next day, walking the streets and the alleys in a six-block radius of the bookstore. Amazingly, on the way back to Books and More, I spotted her in the alley behind Bradford Paints. I was able to lure her to me and get her back to the store, but she disappeared for good a couple of days later, during one of the events we held upstairs in the store. I was sick from food poisoning, resting down in the basement, and did not attend the raucous event.

I wondered, at times, why I'd returned to a wife angry and distant. I had the true love of a cat and dog. The dog and cat and I, we'd made a fine family trio. I feel at times I made a poor decision and should have remained in the woods beyond the time agreed-on by Courtney and I, for in fact we divorced eventually. I never should have taken the cat, the dog, and myself off the limestone ridge by Barton Creek but stayed much longer, perhaps to equal the two years Henry Thoreau spent at Walden Pond. It was the most unique and adventurous thing I ever did in my life.

Yes, I should have remained beyond the six months we planned, continued close to nature and written drafts of a number of books with the free time that comes with low overhead and little need to work. The practice of art requires solitude. That lifestyle involved plenty of exercise and I grew strong and healthy. Skitzy, I still think of you and feel sad about what I did to you. My former wife, Courtney, has been through a number of winters and springs. She was homeless for a while, yet fortunately her nonfiction book was made into a movie script by a writer friend and Courtney got a nice slice of the money. I will always, in some ways, love Courtney because love is forever, but over the sixteen years we'd been together she'd changed, as we all change. When we both got offered much higher-paying teaching jobs a hundred miles away, she refused to leave Austin and remained with her grown kids, even when I suggested I would work and she could stay home and write.

"I don't want to be a faculty wife," she said.

I didn't expect her to be a faculty wife. In fact, that role had died years ago, killed off by feminism.

With Skitzy I experienced the true love of a cat and it was special. Will I know such cat bonding again? When we all had first relocated from the Dobie ranch to the woods, Courtney had insisted on sleeping in her own tent. Minkie dog tried my tent but found it too small. Skitzy, without even asking, took to cuddling next to me at night. The only problem was the cat would get up many times during the night and slip out the small opening in the tent flap I left open for her. Her comings and goings always woke me and some-times made me grouchy the next day.

I remember sitting on a tree stump at the point I called Turkey Vulture Lookout with Skitzy and Minkie. From that point we three could look at the shimmering waters of Barton Creek below, and watch the turkey buzzards coast in the updrafts off the limestone cliffs. I'd write in my journal. The dog or cat would sometimes wander off alone for five or ten minutes. From where we sat you could see nothing but miles and miles of beautiful forested hills, yet Barton Creek mall was but a half-hour walk away.

It was the best of both worlds: civilization and nature. If I wanted some city, I could catch a bus from the mall to downtown. I'd taught the animals to wait for me at the camp without needing to cage them or tie them to a tree.

Chuck Taylor

14

So back in 1988 Courtney and I were promised a half-grown kitten, by this interesting Mormon woman named Ruth I'd met while working the counter of the bookstore. Ruth had been born into a polygamous family near Ogden, Utah, on a sprawling ranch. Her father had four wives, and her mother was the twin of the woman her father had dearly loved, but when he married he had been expected to marry both women on separate days.

One day her father came in the house for supper after repairing sections of broken fence on the ranch. He suddenly realized that it was the anniversary of his marriage to Ruth's mother, so he reluctantly reached into his back pocket and gave his wife his pocketknife. Ruth loved and admired her father, but had no interest in polygamous marriage. Ever since I'd lived in Salt Lake, I'd developed a number of Mormon friends. They seemed pleased to meet a person who knew about their faith and did not judge their practice harshly.

There's much to admire in Mormonism, especially the way they take care of one another. When living in the Salt Lake City avenues area, not far from Temple Square, I'd watch trucks loaded with fresh vegetable deliver food to the old Mormon couples tight on cash. Each neighborhood area "stake" was linked to a farm outside of town. One of the great pleasures of working the counter in the bookstore was I got to talk to all sorts of Austin personalities, like Ruth from a polygamous family. She grew up in an outsider Mormon tradition. Today orthodox Mormons are fervently monogamist.

So, anyway, Courtney found this small backyard house about six months after she abandoned our no-rent tent home in the woods. Getting a place to live out of the bookstore had been a condition of our getting back together. Courtney detested the bookstore basement as much as Skitzy had. Eventually, when I'd been back to the city a month, she and I had managed to scrounge together enough money for the deposit and first month's rent on this quaint hut in the Hyde Park neighborhood in a backyard on Avenue F, close to the Elizabeth Ney Museum. I'd found a fun temporary position working in a downtown print shop.

The hippie property manager of the Hyde Park house was a gentle-spirited guy. The owner of the property had retired to an "art city," San Miguel de Allende in Mexico, where many expatriate Americans live. He'd bought a number of houses in Austin at low prices from the profits he'd made dealing marijuana in the late 1960's, long before the war on drugs was launched. We needed a place for the new kitten we were about to adopt. I was excited.

So we took with us this half-grown kitten from Ruth that we called Lizzie. She was a sweetie who made the move with no trouble. The cat, all black except for four white paws, was developing her climbing skills. She would climb in this bush by our carport onto the low roof of our hut home. Early afternoons when off from work my neighbor Roland and I would talk and watch the cat learning to climb. Roland lived in the larger front house at the front of the property, and had been a plumber back in South Carolina, but now he was studying to get a PhD in botany. He had the short and stocky body that fit the plumber stereotype.

Later I got a better job working all through the night for the Texas School of the Deaf on South Congress in one of their cottages for teenage boys. I tried to sleep during the day in our hut home while Courtney was working at the bookstore, but rarely did I get in more than a couple of hours. I became a walking zombie who couldn't remember the name of the bus I rode home from work in the morning. Courtney complained that when at home she had to be quiet all the time and couldn't invite friends over. I found it highly rewarding to work with the deaf high school boys and became attached to these young men. Deaf may not be the politically correct word. "Hearing impaired" might be considered more politically stylish, but the term, for those of us concerned with language, sounds flat. I learned a few years back that many Indians prefer being called Indians and not Native Americans.

Late afternoons my neighbor Roland would stretch out on a chaise lounge in the front yard with a handkerchief over his bald head, reading *The New York Times*. His wife Sandra would get home from her book designing job at UT Press around 5:30 and then would hit the kitchen to prepare supper. Roland continued to lounge in the front yard.

I sensed Roland's marriage was in worse shape than mine. I could tell by the vibes, but I did not expect Sandra to pack up and move out in the middle of the night, taking all they owned while he was on a research trip to Big Bend National Park to study a fungus that grew on one species of cactus, but that's what she did.

Sandra went into hiding, and the only way Roland could talk to her was when she was at work, and that was for just a few minutes. Sandra had left once before, but Roland had convinced her to come back. This time she had decided she would protect herself from his persuasive words by hiding. Roland had no pets and was alone. He enjoyed the cat Lizzy as much as Courtney and I.

That afternoon outside Roland and I were smiling and entranced, watching the little gal play, as we commented on the perfect spring weather, when suddenly the sun dipped behind in-rolling dark clouds and a sudden gust of wind blew through, shaking up spinners of dust in the gravel driveway. Tree branches began swaying, and large if intermittent raindrops began to splatter the ground.

The kitten, frightened, jumped up on the roof instead of coming down the bush she'd climbed up. Instinct told the cat to look for cover and all she could see was a cone-shaped flue sticking up from our small furnace on the asphalt-shingled roof. Lizzy leaped for cover under the cone and slid down the aluminum pipe right into our hut's furnace. She tried to stop her slide but her claws did no good against the hard aluminum.

Roland and I rushed inside the living room and could make out Lizzy faintly mewing inside the metal wall furnace. She was alive!

But what were we going to do?

"I am a plumber," Roland reminded me, and he rushed to the trunk of his broken-down ancient blue 1973 Honda that his wife had not bothered to take with her. He hauled in a large heavy metal box full of plumbing tools. We began taking the furnace apart. Getting the outside cover off the small gas unit was simple, but once beyond the cover Roland had to get out special tools and extenders to reach bolts deep inside the metal furnace.

Finally he reached the part of the furnace below the aluminum flue. All kinds of parts from the furnace lay on my small living room floor. Roland got the flue open and I reached gingerly inside to pull Lizzy out, who gave a soft mew of relief. The process of freeing the kitten took about two hours.

The poor kitten seemed in shock, so while Roland put the furnace back together, I made up a special soft bed in a cardboard box. I walked down to the convenience store and bought cans of tuna in spring water and fancy canned cat food. Roland hauled his heavy box of tools back to his Honda. We waited and hoped. Perhaps the modern world was too much for cats. They had not only dogs to worry about but the fast growling monsters of metal that rushed up and down streets.

Later, on Roland's advice, I bought the Honda from his former wife for fifty dollars and gave the car to my sons Parker and

Sebastian. Apparently, since Roland's wife had been paying his way through graduate school, Roland, the judge decided, was entitled to nothing. His father fortunately picked up paying his bills and Roland continued in his botany PhD program.

For the next week Courtney and I gave our cat gentle ministrations of attention, but avoided over-hugging and over-cuddling. For a week Lizzy's condition seemed fine. A slide down inside a furnace flue did not seem the kind of activity to cause serious physical injury. We were low on funds as usual and a trip to the vet seemed unnecessary. Just the base cost of a visit would mean we'd be unable to pay next month's rent.

But then one morning I found little Lizzie dead in her bed. I believe she died of shock, not from injuries, unless she had internal injuries we were unaware of. I buried the cat in the backyard, where a month previous I'd sorrowfully buried my border collie Minkie after a wonderful ten years together. We had a small ceremony with a few friends. Courtney lit a candle for Lizzy and I said a quiet prayer. We were both in shock.

Even though I live now in a different town a hundred miles east, when in Austin I'll drive by the house at times where my two animals lay buried, and if no cars are parked in the driveway, I will go up to our former backyard hut and slip around back into the tiny backyard to say a few words for these fine creatures.

I can see now that the lifestyle Courtney and I led could work for dogs, but the moving and our lack of money was not something cats could easily tolerate. But back then I refused to give up. I kept hoping that the next move we made would be our last and we would settle down, stabilize our lives, and work our way out of poverty. Courtney had grown up in a military family that moved all the time. She attended five different high schools. I once read a book called *Military Brats*. The author explained that children from military families often possess rebellious personalities that tend to use moving as a way to run from their problems. I'm not sure where my own rebelliousness came from—perhaps it's due to my father's alcoholism and my mother's long term mental problems that kept her under psychiatric treatment twenty years, till she came to live near me. One is always better at analyzing others than oneself.

I have photos of all the dogs and many of the cats that I've been privileged to enjoy in this life. Some of the photos I have glued to the back of a closet door. Some I keep in a chest with the family photos. From what I've written so far, you might conclude I've been cursed with feline bad luck, but my parents were scientists, and I'm not inclined toward superstition. I've seen many a black cat cross my path, yet I remain healthy and strong, wealthy in life's eccentric gifts of ups and downs, and fairly long lived. Overall I've enjoyed my time on the planet, wrestling with all the diverse angels.

16

The scream of a female cat in heat, the caterwaul, sounds so alien, yet at the same time so human and horrible, no matter how many times you hear it. I've heard it often, since I've lived many years without a car and traveled by foot. At night I've heard the caterwaul coming out of vacant lots and bushes, and thought at first a woman had been pulled off the sidewalk and was being raped and strangled.

Do you have an unfixed female cat in heat? Try to keep the little "slut" inside. "Slut" is a highly charged word for women, a label they especially fear in high school where gossip rages. A cat may be rubbing against your leg, your arm, and the sofa. She may be rolling on her back displaying herself. It's a shame that lovers, I humorously speculate at times, are never that brave, or extroverted enough, to put on such a show—minus the screaming, of course. In the ancient mists of time, long before Puritanism came along to confuse us all, did females—say Egyptian women in the time of the Pharaohs—learn flirtation techniques by imitating cats? Have shards of those sexually charged flirtation techniques traveled down the millennia to be practiced in a more moderate way by present day women? Weaving was learned by observing spiders, it's been claimed. Velcro came from a walk through a field where stickers gathered on the inventor's trousers. Humans have been borrowing from animals and nature since they were hunter-gatherers.

If in the brave new world to come all stray female cats have to be fixed, and only breeders of expensive animals have unfixed cats, the caterwaul—as well as the chorus of howls the males make from nearby bushes in response—could pass from human experience, just as the sight of the stars is now passing from the bright-lit cities.

The caterwaul makes me think of felidomancy. What is felidomancy? It is the practice of prophecy based on the actions and behaviors of cats, be they domestic or wild. The practice of this kind of predictive magic or divination goes back to the Egypt of the Pharaohs, where temple cats, adorned with jewels and magical symbols, were thought to be able to see into the future.

Felidomancy is a worldwide phenomenon. In China it was held that a winking cat meant rain. We all know of the identification of cats, especially black cats, with witches and black magic. Yet, belief about black cats is inconsistent and should make us skeptical. In the United States, Belgium, Spain, and Ireland, black cats are omens of bad luck, but in the British Isles and other parts of Europe a black cat means good luck.

If a lucky bride catches sight of a cat sneezing, she's supposed to have a happy marriage. If a white cat sleeps on your doorstep that means someone in the family is about to get married. If a black cat jumps in the bed of a sick person, that portends death, yet in our culture cats are praised for sitting with the bedridden in nursing homes.

Perhaps all these magical beliefs about cats began with the unearthly scream of the caterwaul—a sound dancing witches might make before dawn in a deep forest, gathered around a large cauldron heated by a log fire.

I don't take to any of these superstitions seriously myself, yet appreciate the fascination humans have for the paranormal. Something appears to be built into our psyches that make us want to believe in magic, but I grew up in a house almost entirely without superstition. I never heard of the evil eye until my mid-twenties when I moved to Texas. My parents, as I may have said, were scientists, medical doctors. Disbelief in superstition is a kind of protection. If I'd believed in the evil eye *mal ojo,* I might have grown pretty paranoid about the dirty looks some folks have shot my way over the years. Yes, I have no truck with superstition, though I know a good cat can't but bring goodness into a life—knock on wood!

Chuck Taylor

17

The beat-hippie 'peace and love' side of my nature, for better or worse, lives hidden inside but remains strong. I was there when Allen Ginsberg coined the phrase "flower power." I carefully read kind Kerouac's favorite gentle book, "The Little Flowers of Saint Frances," and so I have continued to hope that something good can come from my contact with cats. I have faith that my bad fortune with felines will someday evaporate like thick fog under the sun, and cats will begin to see positives in my spirit and not remain hostile or indifferent. Not all cats have disliked my person or acted indifferent. Skitzy and I were superb buddies.

In 1992, while living in an industrial town called Koriyama an hour from Tokyo on the Shinkansen train, my third wife Sayuri and I bought a cat from a Frenchman. He ran a school for teaching (of all things) English to mostly Japanese high school students. Sayuri was an excellent businesswoman and ran a similar business. Her operation also did translations and served as a modeling agency for Westerners to be in Japanese TV commercials. Andre had spent a great amount of time with his kittens. From him I learned that the best way to cultivate a loving cat is to play with the kitten for at least a half hour a day.

"You've got to have free time to devote to the little guy," Andre told me.

Sayuri and I called this timid cat, affectionately and ironically, Shogun. For much of Japanese history the emperor has been a symbolic figure while the actual power for ruling the nation has resided with the Shogun, which originally meant 'slayer of the Ainu.' The Ainu were one of the aboriginal tribes of the islands. The current Japanese migrated to the islands from Korea and elsewhere to intermarry with indigenous tribal groups.

Sayuri and I felt strongly, before our daughter Naomi was born, that Shogun was the center of our hearts, but sadly Shogun grew weaker even as he grew to a full-sized cat. I had more money now and took Shogun to the veterinarian many times—a vet who had gone to the United States and studied at America's number one veterinarian school, Texas A&M, but the good man could find nothing wrong with our dear cat.

Shogun had the small tail of the native Japanese bobtail, and the black and white fur markings of the Maneki Neko. This kind of cat is supposed to sit sometimes with one of its front paws raised. The cat position is held by the Japanese as a good luck sign. I never saw Shogun sit this way.

We were also hearing again, on Japanese television, reports of cats smothering newborn infants. In Japan families often sleep together on the floor in the same room, using futons that are rolled up and put in wall closets during the day. Since our newborn daughter slept on a futon in the same room near us, and Shogun slept in the room also, we began to worry about what might happen.

We also felt that Shogun might do better in a country town with Sayuri's mother. All of her children were raised and she loved cats, did not have one, and might benefit from a cat's company, so we drove out to the town of Nihon-Matsu and gave Shogun away. It was hard parting, but hopefully good for Shogun and good for Sayuri's mother.

Shogun was such a sweet cat. Before he left us he would often sit on my lap while I watched Japanese news with English subtitles, or watched an American language video with Japanese subtitles I'd rented from a nearby video store. Shogun also would perch on my lap while I graded papers. I appreciated that he never once tried to sharpen his claws on the straw tatami mats that serve as floors in most Japanese houses. Shogun loved people and liked to be around them, and became a perfect companion for Sayuri's mother. Perhaps being around a large friendly human animal makes a cat feel secure in a world of larger predators. Shogun got healthier at first, and managed to live on for a year in the large *sake* factory buildings that took up an entire block where my wife Sayuri grew up as a child. The family's living quarters were actually on the second floor of the *sake* factory above the large vats where the alcohol drink ferments. Some call the usually clear beverage "rice wine."

We were broken hearted when Shogun passed. As is the case with many cats, Shogun went off to die alone and not be a bother to others. I believe she choose to go be with the cat gods at the Buddhist temple on a hill a half-block from the *sake* factory. I often hiked in the hilly woods behind the temple and thought I might someday come upon the resting place of sweet Shogun.

My wife Sayuri, as you might have sensed by now, comes from a business family and from the merchant class of Japan. She is a true internationalist in spirit, and spent part of her twenties living on Prince Edward's Island in Canada. She also spent a great deal of time in Los Angeles and New York. Japanese culture inculcates the Japanese at a young age—especially the females—to adore cats. Cats take up less space and don't have to be confined like dogs, a major advantage in a country the size of California yet with half the population of the US. Most homes in Japan have no front or back yards.

In America everyone is familiar with the Japanese cartoon character, "Hello Kitty," and throughout all of Asia porcelain statues of lucky cats, one paw raised, are put at the doors of Asian businesses. Sayuri and I and our small daughter moved to America in late 1994 when Texas A&M/Koriyama, where I worked, shut its doors after a new mayor came into power who refused to support the campus any longer with city funds. I searched to find a new Japanese position but had no luck, probably due to my age. The older you are in Japan, the higher the wages are that you get paid. Universities then preferred young and inexpensive import professors, whenever possible.

My wife compares cats to the Japanese royal family. Sayuri sees a cat's sometime indifference to others as independence and dignity. She finds those qualities inspiring. The Japanese find Western ways of "hug-hug" affection unbecoming and undignified, although they are fascinated by ballroom dancing because their culture avoids physical touch even among those who are married. The dignity and reserve the Japanese admire is similar to the behavior they admire in cats.

"Yes," I reply. "When the Emperor Hirohito toured fire-bombed Tokyo in his limousine during World War II, when he viewed at all the burnt houses and charred bodies, his only questions were about what it all meant to the survival of the royal family."

My wife is silent. She remains, like a cat, above argument.

Even Sayuri, with her cat worship, does not wish to spend large sums on flea treatment for our three cats, so only one of the animals gets to come regularly inside our house and stay for short visits. I call this sleek blue-grey cat "Vomit" when she is throwing up on the carpet (which is often), or "Stubby" when she is not vomiting. The cat was born with a stump of a tail, a birth defect preferred and perfected by cat breeders. Stubby was forced on Sayuri by her former boss, who lives in the country and keeps horses, dogs, and cats.

We already had a cat when Stub arrived, and I don't think my wife would have taken her, except for the fact she did not want to displease her employer. It is not easy for a foreigner, even with a green card, to find enjoyable work, as well as find an employer who will let one take two months off summers to return home to see family.

Stubby spends most of her time when inside the house sleeping in the double bed, often in odd, very trusting and undignified upside-down positions, hidden in the sheets or on a newspaper my wife sets out on the bed. Stub likes to climb inside the bed's box springs and enjoys getting up in the garage attic if I do not remove the ladder soon enough. From inside the box spring and from the attic she must be denied food a few days to get her to come out.

Stub goes out at night, but if she gets hungry she will move around the house from window to window, scratching the screens and thumping like a heavy metal rocker on the windows. Her one-two paw punches I timed once for a full hour. If my wife wakes from sleep, she gets up, lets the cat in the front door, puts food down, waits till she is finished eating, and then puts her back outside in the front yard.

If my wife does not wake and I'm the one who hears the window drumming, I will fill a pan with water, sneak around the outside perimeter of the house in my pajamas, and throw the water at the cat.

This is a satisfying experience. I love to watch Stubby leap off screens backwards in complete surprise. As a man with sleep dysfunctions who constantly struggles to get a good night's rest for the next day's early rise and work, I savor watching Stubby twist and spin to land on her feet, then dash away through the bushes, across the lawn, and up a tree. It means for me no more window pounding and a poor but better night's sleep.

It's more satisfying than smashing a mosquito that's sipping a blood snack from your arm, better than crushing fleeing roaches at 3:00 A.M. rushing helter-skelter across kitchen counters, better than smacking sugar ants with masking tape and flushing them down the toilet! The self-righteousness is wonderful—a true rush— maybe something like what some frenzied TV evangelists might feel when they denounce homosexuals. Animal trainers recommend the water treatment for misbehaving cats, and it doesn't harm anything but the cat's dignity. Sure enough, after about five water treatments, Stubby was cured of the thumping window syndrome.

I don't attribute human levels of cruelty to cats, but Sayuri claims that, in order to get revenge, Stub pissed all over the condensed *Oxford Dictionary* that my grandfather gave me. The samurai of Japan, followers of the Bushido Code, believed revenge to be right action for the warrior. I try to counter my wife's revenge theory with something she saw with her own eyes, that one time Stubby evinced some affection for me.

One winter evening we were in the living room—my daughter, wife, and I watching a DVD—when suddenly Stubby got up from his usual place by the sliding glass doors and ran over and climbed under the blanket I had across myself as I lay on the sofa, suffering, as I often do, from sleep dysfunctions. Stub got down where my toes made the blanket rise up, and cuddled between my feet for warmth.

Sayuri was shocked. She saw it as an unwarranted sign of affection for me, for a person who always verbally insulted her cat. I think Sayrui was a bit jealous. I saw instead a cat that had gotten chilled and was looking for a safe place to warm up. Of course I'm as willing to anthropomorphize as the next person. Perhaps the cat was attempting to make amends. For years behavioral scientists claimed that animals were like robots, and responded only by instinct, a program in their genes. The anthropomorphizers now seem to have been wiser.

Stub also has the remarkable ability to urine on lampshades. Finding a replacement lampshade the right size, color, and shape to fit the lamp that has been attacked requires a vigorous search through many stores. I hate to shop. This is more revenge for my water-throwing torture, Sayuri claims. Stubby has stunk up and stained three living room lampshades. No one has seen her do it. How she gets her derriere up there and aimed in the right direction remains a mystery. I suspect she must run, leap up on the back of a chair or the couch, then leap again and fly by the lampshade, derriere on target with urine spraying out the back.

Six months ago Stubby did the unthinkable. She jumped up on the kitchen counter while Sayuri was chopping root vegetables for supper soup, and brazenly urinated on the portable DVD player Sayuri uses to watch Japanese movies while cooking. Since that moment, Sayuri has grown more vigilant and lets Stubby in the house mainly to eat or when it gets freezing cold at night. Then she sleeps inside under the bed. I am always asking friends if they can smell cat urine when they come to our house because one grows accustomed to the smell. Stubby will go anywhere anytime. She dreams of marking the entire house as hers.

I used to think it was the male cats only who sprayed inside a house to mark territory with an oily, unpleasant scent. We had a young male cat in Salt Lake City, during my marriage to Courtney, who would involuntarily shoot out a squirt of marking scent that would hit a wall or a door jam. He'd then leap into the air with fright and dash into one of the bedrooms to hide under a bed. He was as confused about his blooming sexuality as many a young human male, and seemed to think he was under attack. This cat, who was allowed outside, eventually disappeared. He went feral, I assume, probably to the nearby Mormon cemetery, where many a Mormon patriarch sleeps with his plural wives. How do feral cats survive months in the freezing cold? Huddled inside large tombs? Fortunately, where I live in Texas now, such weather is rare.

One morning, after one of our rare freezes in the winter of 2008, I watched our cat Chibi poke and poke with his paw, with a look both curious and frustrated, at the clear ice filling the outside water bowl next to back door. Chibi had never seen ice before. Are cats born with the instinct to break through frozen layers to reach whatever water may lie below? Being originally from the African desert they need little water. I've seen Stub put both feet in the frozen water dish, push down, and then lick the unfrozen water off the sides that has seeped up around the frozen ice cap.

Feeling a cat's tongue on a finger, as the cat presumably licks for salt, reminds me always of a line from a poet whose name I've forgotten, how a cat's tongue feels not like fine sandpaper but like "Melba toast." When Sayuri spots one of the cats trying to get water, she will often hurry outside and pour warm water onto the ice. On our rare freezing Texas nights, we turn on a radiant heater in the garage for the cats who stay outside. On such nights, cats Chibi, Pounce and Stubby, along with my dog Biscuit, used to huddle in a distance circle around the radiance, at peace for once.

Humans have created global warming and nuclear bombs, yet I doubt it would be a safer world if cats ruled. On normal days, our cats "entertain" themselves by constantly jockeying for control of territory. Exact boundaries may shift slightly, but main areas seem to be established. Chibi seems to control the garage and backyard. Pounce owns the driveway, the south side of the house, and the front bushes. Stub gets to come inside and controls the back patio and the north side of the house. Warfare rarely breaks out that might redesign each cat's territorial map. What I dream of seeing is our cats forming a unified force of three to repel big animal assaults from beyond our property lines. These animals often waltz in late at night to eat cat food, dog food, or whatever else they can find. I must keep birdseed in a metal garbage can because squirrels will bite through a plastic one.

I once watched cats on TV that peacefully perched on stations built at different levels inside a small screened-in porch with a good outdoor view. They rotated their stays on high, middle, and low perches with each other, supposedly without getting into spats. Is this a utopian fantasy, or could the different perches represent to cats their instinctual practice of sharing a large tree, and rotating with each other branches high and low, so that each cat enjoys roughly the same opportunities to catch birds and insects for supper?

A cat democracy in the trees?

18

THE ONE TRUE CAT. By "true" I don't mean to imply anything about fidelity. None of us, I hope, wants love with a cat and only a cat, no matter how much we come to care for that special cat. We need others in our lives.

It's true that I've grown skeptical about most cats as I am skeptical about most dogs. Some cats appear at times lazy to me and act at best with dignified indifference toward those who care for them. Love has a practical aspect and requires exchange. I mow the lawn, do house repairs, maintain the car, and hold a full-time job. Sayuri works part-time and does almost all of the cooking and laundry. We both straighten and clean.

My golden retriever Biscuit once guarded our house, killed rats when they got in the garage, warned me of possible intruders by barking, and greeted me with great enthusiasm when I came home. For these services, and also out of love, I happily provided food, water, companionship, and plenty of petting. We both got our exercise together, walking at the Lick Creek County Park where we enjoyed the beauty of a wilder world.

I drove three hours east to the Davy Crockett National Forest to pay four hundred dollars to a forest ranger for Biscuit when he was a puppy. Biscuit was supposed to be my daughter Naomi's dog. Naomi was supposed to learn responsibility and caring, but the dog grew larger than the standard retriever. Naomi became frightened and I became the primary care giver. No large animal like Biscuit would ever be seen as cute by my daughter and inspire her to love.

I wonder sometimes if she'll fall in love and marry a cute, small guy. If he's a good man, that's fine with me.

Golden retrievers are consistently rated as intelligent as border collies and are patient and gentle with children. Unlike most cats, Biscuit loved to go on trips both long and short in my Mazda pickup, where, until the speed got up to around fifty and the wind got to blowing hard, he rode with his head out the window sniffing the spicy marvelous smells that shot by.

Biscuit was a special kind of golden retriever known as a red-golden because of the reddish tinge of his coat. His favorite activity was diving into the water and swimming out to fetch the large sticks I'd throw far out into a large pond hidden deep in the wilds of Lick Creek Park.

Sayuri, my cat lover Sayuri who never had a dog until Biscuit, remarked one night, when a Christian Japanese friend came over to visit, that Biscuit was a kinder, sweeter and more loving creature than any of us, and more like Jesus than any man she had met who considered himself Buddhist or Christian. She was feeling especially sad about Biscuit since his sudden passing away. Sayuri attended Catholic school throughout her childhood in Japan and knows much about Jesus and Christian theology, although she remains firmly a Shinto-Buddhist, with an altar where she says prayers for her ancestors every day.

Biscuit was a superior being. If he'd had the ability to take his native goodness actively out into the world, I'd rate him with the Dalai Lama, Nelson Mandela or Martin Luther King. What cat could be compared to Christ? Sayuri mentioned a famous statue of a dog named Hachiko that once waited years for his master to return at Ueno Station in Tokyo after his master died of a sudden heart attack.

We were all sitting around the dinner table in our College Station house, sipping bubble soda through a wide straw with little round balls of tapioca floating in each bottle. Somehow the little balls could be sucked up the wide straw with the liquid. Sayuri's Japanese Christian friend Tomoe always carried in her arms a tiny fluffy white-haired dog. As soon as Stubby cat saw it, he headed for his favorite hiding spot inside the box springs of the bed. The cat had torn open his own hatch in the box springs. We'd repaired it once but that just led him to claw open a new one.

Many a cat can be compared to an expensive, beautiful vase one might keep on the mantel above the fireplace. You enjoy the still beauty of the vase as you enjoy the still sleeping beauty of an indifferent cat. Many a cat is an aesthetic pleasure, like a lovely Renoir print mounted on a wall. Oh oh. It sounds as if I've just about given up on cats here. Maybe I have.

Unless there was a war raging in their lord's territory, the Samurai in Japan did little work beyond training, and sat around, often drinking, with little to do but sing songs, attend tea ceremonies, seduce women, and recite the haiku they'd written. They were noble, beautiful loungers as cats are noble beautiful loungers and vases are noble beautiful loungers. Since vases are inanimate objects, lacking arms and legs and requiring no feeding, their constant lounging might be a shade more tolerable than cats.

Still, I know some cats are capable of more. Life can be better and some cats can be affectionate and loving, especially if you spend a lot of time playing with them when kittens. When we got Stubby we bought a plastic stick with colored feathers on the end. She enjoyed playing with this toy for about five minutes. We also dangled colored yarn in front of her face and dragged it across the carpet. Perhaps we did not do these activities long enough. In my life I've been blessed with two loving cats, Skitzy and Shogun, but sadly they died young. Just how much time does one need to spend with a kitten to develop a loving cat?

I hope—I will myself to believe—that the young in this often-cruel world of ours do not need to die young. I don't accept the old saw that the good die young. Someday the right kitten will meow my name and step forward to bless my life and the lives of others. I hang onto this faith. I've always been discriminating (a nice word for "hard to please").

On the main highway coming into the small East Texas town of Edgewood from the West, up a small hill, sat an empty home with a "For Sale" sign. The last of member of the family had passed six months ago, but so far no one had shown interest in purchasing the old house. I couldn't understand why. The price was a reasonable ten thousand dollars (this was 1979), and the house and property were in half-decent shape on attractive, tree-shaded land.

I walked around the house one spring day back in 1979. We were thinking of buying the place, since it was on the main highway, to convert it into a record store and Texana bookshop. I noticed a rusted old air conditioner sticking out of a kitchen window. On top of the air conditioner sat a grey cat sunning itself. A hole in the window screen allowed the cat to slip into the empty house, which the feline did when he or she spotted me approaching.

Once again I realized that many cats are more in love with territory than with the people on the territory who happen to feed them. The cat was in perfectly good health and spirits in spite of the loss of those who had cared for the creature. Either the cat was surviving on mice and bugs, or it had found another human food source down the highway.

I'm not convinced that all cats can tell the difference between people. Many cats can and do, of course, but for some cats people are viewed mostly as a FOOD SOURCE, and few if any distinctions are made. When people move to another part of the world where a different ethnicity dominates, they also have trouble making distinctions. My daughter, when she came back to the United States after a year on a foreign exchange, thought that all Euro-Americans looked alike. When I first arrived in Japan, all the Japanese seemed to look alike.

Dogs are loyal to the pack and to the leader of the pack. Cats are loyal to a place. I imagine cats as once arboreal creatures, perched on branches of trees in the ancient hot evenings of Egypt. They would perch, quiet and still on branches, hidden by leaves, waiting for birds or large insects to land within pouncing distance. I imagine cats always patient in trees, still as sleep, eyes intently open, waiting for the next meal. Cats needed to be still to conserve energy and catch prey. Cats hunted mostly under the cover of night when most birds and bugs were sleeping.

Have humans, by providing regular meals, ruined cats, turned them into nearly useless objects like vases? Are cats depressed? Is that why they often sleep most of the day away? They may both love and hate us. We've made their lives easier, but being on welfare doesn't always endear the receiver to the one providing the handout. I realize it's not pleasant to think about this possibility, but perhaps we humans can do things to keep our cats' minds active and their bodies lively. I know you love your cat and are concerned for its welfare.

Chuck Taylor

19

In the year 2002, Pounce was booted out of her litter, while still a kitten, by her mother—from their lair under a house down the street. I often spotted mother sunning in the front lawn about a block away when I walked the golden retriever. Pounce managed to pry open the back door of an old green van I parked in the driveway for storage. It was cold and raining the night she moved in seeking cover.

Sayuri didn't want another cat. We'd had two cats already and something sad had happened to one of them. One puss we'd inherited when we moved into the house in 1994 was picked up in 1999, without our knowledge, by the city's animal control division. They decided Totoro was too old and needed to be "put down" (as they say). Totoro did sometimes drool a bit and did not see well, but she seemed content enough and displayed no symptoms of contagious disease. All these actions were taken without consultation or even a phone call.

It all sounds a bit police state, don't you think, seizing an animal and killing it without consulting with the owners? I live in an conservative city that was once a part of a slave confederacy, with one former plantation within its present city limits and other former cotton plantations nearby. Many fine people live here, and I have learned from them, yet even some of the natives will joke that the town is so boring that the only entertainments are the movies and the mall. That's all. A boring place, a place where new ideas are not coming in frequently, tends to not change with the times. Our town seems not to have heard of the animal rights movement. In contrast, seaport cities like San Francisco, New Orleans, New York, Vancouver, Los Angeles, Galveston, and even Chicago on Lake Michigan, can easily stay fresh and adapt because new ideas are coming with new nationalities arriving on boats.

We held a ceremony for Totoro cat in a front yard flowerbed. Sayuri painted a large stone I fetched from a nearby creek bed in Totoro's honor. This gave some relief to our then eight year-old daughter Naomi, who believed our cat that now lay under the stone in the earth had died of natural causes. I didn't have the heart to tell her that the city had confiscated Totoro and put her down.

It was our daughter's first death.

I remembered the summer of 1996 when we took Totoro to a cattery because my wife and daughter were headed to Japan to visit relatives and I was taking a camping trip through the Southwest. The cattery was in a 1950's ranch style house on the corner of Carson and Cavett in an older section of Bryan, the twin city of College Station. We were nervous about leaving the old cat alone and away from the house, but decided she would be too much for a neighbor to feed and watch over.

Seeing the inside of the cattery did little at first to calm our worries. It consisted of rows of cat cages one on top of the other. At least the room had plenty of windows to allow natural sunlight to flood in. The lady who operated the business lived on site in the house and seemed patient and pleasant. The cats in the cages— maybe about ten—seemed content with where they were. They could see each other yet were protected inside the cages. None paced the parameters of cages meowing with discontent. The cattery ended up seeming a good place for Totoro.

I worried about the cat on my southwest adventures to Big Bend, to Indian Hot Springs, to the Guadalupe Mountains, to El Paso to see friends, and to Bisbee, Arizona, a blossoming art colony we were considering moving to. How would Totoro–a mostly outside but sometimes inside cat–take to being locked in a cage all the time? I had learned not to allow myself to get too profoundly attached to cats, if I can help it, because they live short lives and my luck with cats seemed not good, yet I try to treat cats with fairness and kindness. The cat we'd inherited when we bought the house was not much interested in people, yet she'd lived at the house first, before we arrived. She did not understand the odd human concept of property ownership determined by deeded sheets of paper.

How could we dare think of getting rid of her?

I had made efforts to get to know Totoro, to play with her and hold her, but was rebuffed every time, and so were my wife and daughter. Since the cat did not like me, I did not see much reason to feel much for her. This was not true for Sayuri and Naomi. They are better people who continue to love cats in spite of their indifference. Just think what that kind of love could accomplish if these two great ladies went to work for Oxfam or the Bill and Linda Gates Foundation.

When I picked up Totoro from the cattery at the end of my southwest adventuring, before my daughter and wife got back from Japan, she looked great. What a surprise! She was calm, of the same weight, and just as well groomed as ever. Living in a cage for a month didn't seem to bother her at all. Perhaps she liked the other cats around her as company, since they were in cages too and she did not need to worry about any of them attacking her.

Life will often surprise you. That's one of the things that makes life fun. I don't believe I've ever spent more than a couple of hours bored. Totoro didn't seem to recognize who I was but she didn't scratch or try to get loose when I picked her up and put her in the cat carrier. She hunkered down on the drive home and didn't make a sound. Once I let her out of the cage at the house, she seemed to know where she was and went back to her old routine of mostly sitting under the front yard Texas sage.

But anyway—to return to the new cat, Pounce—I started leaving food for her in the old van. Sayuri, still in grief over the city's killing of the inherited house cat Totoro, grumbled but took no contrary actions. It's just an outside cat, I told her—mainly a wild cat. I'd take care of the little one. That meant, as far as I was concerned, I'd put daily food and water down when I fed the dog.

She was such a little cat. I didn't think she could go into heat and get pregnant. But soon the males started to gather and howl from the bushes. Too young, I told myself. I've always had quarrels with the concept of "fixing" animals. To have quarrels with castration takes little sympathetic imagination. Few humans wish to be castrated or have a hysterectomy.

Cats, I had not yet grasped, can multiply like rats. One female cat can couple with multiple males in less than one night. That accounts for the variety you find in coloration in a single litter. Different sperm from different males fertilizes different eggs. Oh well, no reason to anthropomorphize and be priggish about the sexual practices of a different species.

The kittens were cute, the four of them, all curled up in the green van with their mother. I provided extra food, milk, and water for the mom and her new family. I left her to her privacy for about a week. I felt that was needed. I remembered when I was four in Chicago, dropping a kitten while holding her in my arms. I still saw that kitten's head hitting the cement floor, her single spasm, and then her stillness.

But then I opened the green van to check on the mother and babies. I was greeted by the thick smell of death. All four of the babies were curled up dead, just inside the van's back doors. Some cat, either the mother or a tom, had bitten each in the head, squashed their skulls. They did not want any further competition for the area's territory.

When I saw that grisly scene I did not know that a male tom could be the responsible party. I assumed the mother had killed her own children. I sparked with anger and yelled at Pounce as she fled up the driveway toward the garage.

"Child killer!"

I tried to make up to Pounce later, after I buried the kittens in the back yard without telling my daughter. I would ride my exercise machine in the garage while watching the news on a ancient black and white portable I found at a garage sale for five bucks.

While I rode up and down on the machine, Pounce would shyly try to climb off the ping-pong table onto my moving legs. She was making friends. We were making up, I thought. I'd stop riding the machine, sit still, and watch the news. Soon the cat was curled in my lap. I was worried my golden retriever Biscuit would grow jealous, since he was still alive at the time and also in the garage, but he was a mellow dog. Biscuit didn't bark or come over to sniff and find out what was happening.

Then one evening Pounce bit me, deep, on the wrist.

Apparently I wasn't getting the message. We'd moved the food bowl into the garage onto the ping pong table we rarely used. Food lay in her bowl, but after biting me and breaking the skin, she leaped off my lap onto the table and scuttled over to the bowl. She desired fresh food, not the scattered dry pebbles left over from morning that had probably lost their tasty scent.

I climbed off the exercise bike, bent over, and gave her soft slap in the face. I knew about cat diseases, and with my sleep dysfunctions I was not sure how resilient my immune system was. After that, I went inside and washed with disinfectant soap where she'd broken the skin and blood was coming out. Sayrui had spent one feverish day in bed when the old house cat Totoro had bitten her before he died. I wanted to avoid "cat scratch fever," a concept I once knew of only from a Ted Nugent song and never considered literal, just a metaphor for unhappy love. I should have known something literal always lies behind a good metaphor.

Sayuri was not angry long with Totoro for biting her. That is her Japanese way. Our other cats since then have both scratched and bitten her. She claims that cat biting and scratching is left over kitten behavior, and is a cat's unique way of showing affection. I have a deep admiration for Sayuri's faith in cats. I wonder if faith is a precondition for unconditional love, and I often yearn to be less male, less Protestant, and less judgmental. But then I come back to myself, and it seems my wife has such a great capacity for denial.

My eldest son Parker lives on a musician's collective south of the city of Austin, Texas. A few years later, I was spending the night on a futon in the living room of the largest house on the two-acre wooded property. When I first lay down to sleep the terrier Woody and the cat Jamison were sharing the futon with me, but Woody decided to go up the stairs and sleep with the couple on the second floor he knew better. That was OK with me because he was constantly scratching his fleas. Black and white Jamison stayed on the futon. She was amazingly comfortable with a huge pile of blankets on top of her that cold December night, but she didn't like me to move around much.

To get me to lie still Jamison bit me, one time during the night, on the big toe, and later, closer to morning, on the left arm, but when Jamison put her teeth to my skin she did it in a warning yet playful way, never hard enough to break the skin. Cat fanciers call this kind of bite the inhibited bite. A cat who stays in the litter long enough will learn this restrained bite. Kittens who leave the litter too early, or have a human around who plays rough house, usually bite hard.

My son Parker told me that Jamison sometimes nips him on his bare heels while sleeping. Jamison one weekend was acting weird, moving from room to room, meowing a lot, not his usual laid back self. Parker's lovely lady was out of town, on tour with her folk music group. When my son told her about Jamison on the phone, she told him to take five minutes to play with Jamison on the bed and he'd be happy.

I wonder if geckos— the small, light green lizards with padded toes that can strut up windows or walls—have as much personality variation as cats? We seem to assume that a creature with a small head and brain will be stupid, but this may not be the case.

Chuck Taylor

20

The Japanese, as I have mentioned, seem to all adore cats. Cat love is set deep in their characters, although with humans you always get exceptions. The Japanese believe strongly in non-verbal communication and are convinced they can read cat minds. Biting I suppose is a form of non-verbal communication. Probably the most famous and widely read Japanese novel is by Soseki Natsumi. Published first in a single volume edition in 1911, it is an entire novel told from the point of view of a cat. The book is called in English translation *I am a Cat*. So popular was the novel that the author Soseki wrote two sequels.

Cats, I earlier mentioned, will come sit on the beds of the ill in nursing homes shortly before the elderly die. I've seen it on television news reports, and I assume the scenes are not staged. A cat can provide the comfort of a living presence when family and friends and nursing personnel are busy and unable to be with the dying. Could cats see the souls of the soon to be departed, and use their presence to help souls cross the threshold to the next world? Cats are always careful about crossing thresholds. I used to give cats a gentle shove in the rear with my foot if they waited too long to go out a door—until I realized they were checking for predators before leaving a house for the unpredictable outside.

The ancient Egyptians worshiped cats and slaughtered them in honor of their mummified high priests and pharaohs. They did the slaughtering in high numbers. Does any culture eat cats as the Koreans eat dogs and the French eat horses? I have sampled a little horse and dog, to get an idea of the flavor.

I must admit I am curious about the taste of cat. I'd prefer baked to fried.

Could I actually eat leg or breast of cat?

Is there enough meat on the animal?

No, I couldn't. I was a vegetarian for over a year because I considered it healthier and did not wish to kill animals, but then I grew weak and eventually ill. A physician told me that my metabolism requires meat and rather unhappily I returned to a light meat diet, mostly of fish and chicken.

Pardon me, reader. I hope I did not offend too much discussing the eating of animal flesh. The Hindu may feel as unhappy about our beef diet as we do with those who eat dog. A little barbarian humor is one way I choose to deal with cat challenges. What people will eat is largely determined by culture. When in Japan I was served and tasted numerous blooming flowers when dining in fancy restaurants. Other customers were eating the flowers so I guessed they were not poisonous. I also ate fried grasshopper.

21

Perhaps I've gotten carried away with my food speculations. I don't always have difficulties with cats, and cats don't always have difficulty with me. I may not be always the easiest dude to be around, but then who is? We have three cats in the house these days that Sayuri and daughter Naomi love deeply. I love them the best I know how.

The city tells me we have the legal limit of animals allowed in a single family residence, and I can't get another dog to help fill the void left by the passing of my golden retriever. I don't believe all dogs go to heaven. The pair of pit bulls down the street who broke through a fence and killed their own father, they're headed for hell— or at least purgatory—but my red-golden Biscuit is certainly up above now that he is gone.

Chibi, our wildest cat, will rarely let any human touch him. As I write now in a chair with my computer on my lap, it is an early Saturday morning in 2010. Later I need to drive my daughter Naomi to her high school for a Saturday Student Council carwash fund raiser. Stubby and Chibi are giving each other alternating playful and hostile stares through the sliding glass doors in the living room. Stubby grows tired of the game and walks over to the couch and puts her paws up, claws extended, to do some sharpening. I give him a gruff "Ah!" and she changes her mind and skips away. Sometime later today she'll guiltlessly attempt the same thing, whether I am sitting nearby or not.

When returning from taking my daughter to school, I pass by

Pounce asleep close to the prickly pear cactus Sayuri planted beneath my daughter's bedroom window, which faces the street, to protect from intruders. Pounce raises her head and I bend over and scratch her under the ears. Once inside I lie down for a nap. I've forgotten I left Stubby inside. The cat comes to the door of the bedroom and meows once for me to get up. She's bored, grown tired of sleeping, and her mind has turned to her other main interest, food.

Stubby knows I am a light sleeper. I come out of a dream about an old poet friend, now deceased, and start jotting the dream down in my journal, but the cat meows more. This time her meow is more insistent, more like a command, so I climb out of bed and start down the hall to the kitchen. I put down the dry food that she doesn't like. She wants the moist food in the refrigerator, but I ignore her and pick up a book in the far end of the living room.

Stubby sits by the food dish, determined to wait. She does it with the quiet dignity of a professional beggar, but finally gives up and moves to the back door. She then mews twice and I get up to let her out. As the cat goes out there's a tense interaction between Stub and Chibi, but they manage to get by each other with no hissing or fighting. I saw a woman at the local Target store last week wearing a red t-shirt with the following message:

> SCHEDULE FOR THE DAY
> 1)Let cat out.
> 2)Let cat in.
> 3)Let cat out.
> 4)Etc.

Your best chance for giving Chibi a loving pet is when he is crouched over the food bowl in the garage, but the muscles in her back will remain tense. Chibi, who is mostly white and grey and is the second cat that wandered up to the house, catches mice and birds. He toys with them on the back patio before killing them. Chibi has large, deep, green amber eyes. They are powerfully hypnotizing.

Do cats understand, in such moments, what terror and suffering they are inflicting on another creature? It's hard to believe that the same animal who lies patiently with patients close to death in nursing homes can also toy with birds and mice for hours before killing them.

Cats are as paradoxical as humans, who one moment are dropping a bomb from a drone on an Afghani house, killing the extended family inside suspected of "harboring" a terrorist, and then the next moment are flying an Iraqi child to France for special surgical treatment of a rare eye condition. The latter I saw on TV and suspect it was true but in part a public relations stunt staged by the US military. If not arranged, TV cameras and reporters would not be present.

I once ordered a cat video over the Internet for Chibi, and took it along with a small color TV with a built-in video player out to the garage for Chibi to watch. Since Chibi is fascinated with birds, I thought he'd enjoy watching the birds sing and dance in trees on the video. Maybe it would take his mind off torturing and killing.

I set the color TV on the ping pong table away from the cat food and water bowls. I put a blanket down about six inches from the TV. I shook the food container and Chibi jumped up on the ping pong table thinking I'm about to put out fresh food into the bowls—or perhaps I'm about to provide something different, more scrumptious like wet meaty cat food? Cats are not vegetarians. They need a spot of meat each day to stay healthy.

I've got my garden gloves on and had on my winter coat (it was winter) to protect against scratches. I grab Chibi, put her in the catch cage we use to take our cats to the vet or on trips, and set the cage on the blanket in front of the TV. Then I turned off the pause button. I tap on the glass of the TV to get Chibi's attention focused on the screen. I spent about fifteen minutes tapping on the glass trying to get the cat to focus.

Chibi doesn't get it. The skipping of the birds on the screen, all the sprightly chirping sounds, doesn't interest her. Not even the brilliant red male cardinal hopping in low branches engaged the cat's eye. I leave her there and go back inside the house for an hour. I go back to the garage after watching the news and Chibi meows mournfully to be liberated. I open the door and she scrambles away.

Ah well. I feel for cats. They certainly are beautiful animals. Some dog breeds are dumb and ugly, but I don't think I ever saw an ugly cat unless it might be some of the specialized designer breeds made for cat shows. The shape and look of current Siamese cats—so different from the two I suffered climbing on my head in my twenties—seem ugly to me. Hairless cats don't appeal at all.

Sometimes cats have strange markings. People out of habit will reject a cat because black, somewhere deep in their minds, is associated with witches. But unusual markings may draw others and make them more curious and sympathetic. Just as no person should be judged by skin color, so no cat should be judged by fur color or pattern, or even for lack of fur. It's the inside that matters most. Even Stubby with her nub of a tale is attractive and interesting. I am amazed she can balance so perfectly without a tale as a counterbalance. Walking a fence, she seems to me a tightrope walker performing without a balancing pole. Stub is quite the clean cat, and it is fun to watch her lick her paws till they are wet and then wash her face. I suspect she has hair balls in her belly that cause her to vomit often. They are a result of her frequent grooming.

So you see, cats are part of the rhythm of my life, but don't they get bored sleeping all the time? I've never seen cat legs twitching like dog legs when they are dreaming. I have heard cats softly snoring.

Do cats dream? Don't their brains shrink after the playful kitten period passes and they start sleeping up to seventeen hours a day with no work of hunting to do? Maybe that's why they get along with people in nursing homes. Perhaps some cats are like old people sleeping in chairs, mentally fading away.

NOTE TO BRAIN RESEARCHERS:

Study the chemistry of the cat brain to determine if there is a chemical, or a complex of chemicals, that prevent atrophy in the cat brain, despite the cat's long periods of inactivity. Assuming no side effects are found, this chemical or complex of chemicals might be given to the elderly to keep their minds functioning when they are inactive, due to illness or due to the loss of the use of legs or other muscles.

NOTE TO READERS:
I am not joking.

Loving dogs ain't always easy, especially if you have a dog that likes to dig its way out of the back yard and run off. There can at times be something about their adoration and slavishness that is more than a tad disgusting. They would be perfect citizens of totalitarian societies. They will faithfully perform good or evil acts, with no moral compunction, based on the orders of their masters. The Nazis knew this and used dogs accordingly. The English writer D.H. Lawrence would complain in poems about his dog's lack of discrimination in giving love, even as Lawrence adored his dog.

Ah but dogs are loyal. Dogs are loving. With their spectacular noses, dogs rescue people from collapsed buildings all over the world. Rescue dogs will grow overwhelmed by the suffering they encounter and must be played with to cheer them up. Dogs do have a sense of right and wrong, at least from within the parameters of the ethical system a master instructs. Throughout history dogs have protected us, pulled our sleds through snow, hunted with us, and herded our sheep. Civilization could not have developed without dogs.

Loving cats is more challenging, a true wrestling with angels. If we don't have a grain silo in our back yards being threatened by mice or birds, what can they do for us that a mousetrap can't do? Mousetraps also don't require much food or care, and they don't fill up the home up with shed hair.

Maybe cats are as hard to love as humans.

I did meet a painter who lives on a farm outside of Elgin, Texas. She told me her farmer husband says cats can come inside when they start paying taxes.

"We like feral cats," she says. "They get the rats. They keep back the copperheads and the coral snakes. They don't eat them but they like to kill them."

Whether I've been good with cats or bad, whether I am a person naturally liked by cats or a person naturally feared or disliked, I have nevertheless taken time to preserve in words here many of the cats of my life, and preserve the complex, paradoxical spirit of cats. Oliver Cromwell, the great general and ruler of Puritan England, told his portrait artist to paint him with "warts and all." I have done that here with myself and with "my" cats.

We've seen enough namby-pamby cat books, have we not? You've read them. I've read them. The never ending tone of perky optimism could send a sane man leaping off the Cliffs of Dover into the cold waters of the English Channel. This isn't exactly a cat book anyway. It's a memoir with cats.

22

My wife Sayuri is so attached to Stubby cat that she carries on long conversations with the animal, especially in the morning when she is feeding all cats and preparing for work. Often I get out of bed before Sayuri and the cats get to enjoy a double feeding. It's our little secret, the cats and I.

Sayuri also likes to talk in Japanese to the cat while the cat lies on the bed and Sayuri watches her satellite Japanese TV programs. If I start, in a teasing way, insulting Stub for vomiting and pissing in our house, or for lying around and doing nothing, my wife warns me to expect revenge. Sayuri so loves Stubby that she has suffered through bouts of ringworm—one spot on the neck and one on each hand—from the cat.

I tell my wife that Stub doesn't understand English. The cat only speaks Japanese. As mentioned before, we have three cats, and Stub is the only cat allowed inside for long, but there's also Pounce and Chibi or "Wild Cat" as I call him. Pounce the cat that moved into the green van seems to move around stoned all the time. She acts like a marijuana pothead and makes me feel as if it's still 1968.

Pounce often sleeps in the front bushes or under one of the cars in the driveway. I always honk to make sure she has gotten out of the way. She's so oblivious it would be easy to murder her by tire. Pounce—named by my daughter—has wonderful coloring. She's black with paint-like splotches of orange from the tip of her tail to her nose. Some call this fur design tortoise shell. She looks a bit like a Jackson Pollock painting. Once in a while, walking to the car from the house, I'll run across Pounce lounging in the sun on the lawn. She'll roll over and respond to a little belly rubbing and ear scratching.

Stubby used to be the biggest, baddest cat—sole cat of the inside world, and dominant outside. But Chibi is no longer a juvenile and can easily beat Stub in a fight. For a week now, this summer of 2010, Stubby has been trying to stay mostly inside, nursing a large wound on her stomach from Chibi. Chibi's back haunches now resemble the legs of a body builder.

Chibi, as I mentioned earlier, will occasionally catch birds and kill them—even hummingbirds. She often catches and toys with the light green geckos common to the Brazos Valley of Texas where we live. These lizards are a marvel, and can even walk up a glass window. Their paws contain super-microscopic hairs that use a special molecular gravitational force. Scientists hope to design adhesives that work the same way. The squirrels gather under my bird feeders to eat the sunflower seeds the birds have dropped. They have not yet figured out how to get on the bird feeders. When Chibi spots a squirrel he will confidently chase the animal away.

I'm remembering early 2009, before my Biscuit, my beautiful Golden Retriever of twelve years, passed away. Biscuit used to break up fights between Stub and Chibi. Chibi, then a juvenile, would sleep on Biscuit's bed for protection against the larger Stubby. What it is about Stub that wins my wife's affections is hard to fathom. I think it must be the cat's beauty. She has a lovely light grey coat, with four white feet and a diamond white spot on her chest. I don't know whether to call Stubby or any of the other cats she, he, or it since they are now all fixed. I try to call them by what gender they were born to before going under the knife, but at times, you may have noticed, I get confused.

When Sayuri and I drove down to far south Texas to see my second son Sebastian in the spring of 2009, Sayuri didn't mind leaving the other two cats behind with food and water set out aplenty in the garage, but she feared leaving Stubby. I reminded her that cats did not travel well but she insisted on bringing her favorite. Sayuri worried especially about the two newly arrived pit bulls living in the next yard, even though I informed her they were females and probably not aggressive.

Stub traveled the long seven-hour drive inside a special new and larger cat cage my wife purchased at a pet store. Once we got there, late in the evening, she snuck the cage into our downtown Edinburgh Echo Motel room and let the cat out. The next morning, before we went to visit my son and his family, Sayuri had trouble getting Stubby out from under the Echo Motel bed. It took all three of us lying on the floor, working from three sides of the bed, to accomplish this task. Luckily the front part of the bed faced the wall.

Sayuri also let the cat out at my son Sebastian's house. Somehow, after dark, Stubby got out the door into the big fenced-in front yard where two large mongrels make their home. The dogs spotted Stubby and took off after her in what I am sure she knew was a life or death race. The cat beelined for our car, according to my grandchildren. She got up underneath and then worked her way into a hidden spot somewhere around the engine. The dogs stood and barked by the car and tried getting underneath, but could not find a way to reach her.

"Don't worry," I joked to Sayuri, "when I turn on the engine things will heat up fast and she will zip out."

"Well, she could get sliced in half by a moving part," my son Sebastian, the truck driver, explained.

After trying for an hour to find the cat, Sayuri promised five dollars to whichever grandchild could get the cat out of its hiding place around the car's engine.

"You're the only ones who can do it," she said. "You've all got small hands."

About an hour later my grandson Ricardo came in the house carrying the missing cat. I was amazed. My wife was so relieved and happy to pay the five dollars. In fact, she gave all four grandchildren five dollars because they'd all worked so hard helping to locate the cat. I had to admit that Stubby must possess high survival intelligence. With no big trees in south Texas to scale and escape dogs, she instantly knew our budget Korean car was her best chance.

23

The great Athenian philosopher Plato, in his dialogue *Symposium*, presents a hilarious story about the origin of humans. According to Aristophanes (an actual Greek playwright put into Plato's fictional dialogue), when the human race was first created, humans were in the shape of a circle. Humans were complete beings (the circle is the shape symbolizing perfection) who had four legs and four arms and traveled fast by rolling like a ball, but then these over-confidant souls challenged the powerful god Zeus, who tossed down lightning bolts and put them in their places by splitting them in half.

Plato's story attempts to explain why humans are always discontented. Humans spend much of their lives painfully, desperately, and often hilariously, searching for their other half so they can again be rejoined in perfection.

The problem is, most humans marry the first "other half" that shows them attention and affection, rather than finding the actual half part that fits them best. Thus the world ends up with many imperfect marriages and divorces. People are impatient. They are sexually frustrated. They can't wait out the years until they find that better match, a more compatible mate. If they wait too long, maybe they'll grow too old and not find anyone.

I find the romantic yearning the Aristophanes myth pokes fun at much more tragic than humorous. Blind faith in romance, as the source of happiness on earth, leads to much human pain. The tragic failures of love get told over and over in songs and movies, yet few seem to get the message and wise up. Our hormones keep us blind. Of course we were never round and we were never split in half. Soul mates don't exist and we can't be made whole by romantic love.

Aristophanes was a funny guy, a classic writer of incredible comic plays like the wonderful *Lysistrada*, where the Spartan and Athenian women try to stop the war between their city states by denying their warrior husbands sex. Aristophanes liked to joke around to make serious points. I'll emphasize the playwright's notion by slightly rewriting the words the Rolling Stones sang, "You can't get no satisfaction." The romantic yearning for perfection is real enough, but no perfect soul mate exists out there for you.

Sorry Charlie. Sorry Charlene.

Conflict will always happen when you live with any creature on the planet for more than six months, but accepting this fact doesn't mean that there are no souls out there who are more compatible and others who are less compatible. The US Census Bureau estimates world population to be 6,780,527,459. Certainly there's more than one person out there for you! All you need is money for travel and an ability to learn languages.

It is good to take your time and find a person who shares your interests and may share some of your frailties. If you are a messy person, for instance, it might be wise to get together with another messy person. If you are a spontaneous free thinker, you might be better off *not* getting together with a disciplined career military officer. Ah but we don't like being lonely, and can't wait forever, can we? One of my doctor friends returned to Germany because he could not find a spouse in the United States. A colleague said he should have lowered his standards.

Can you find a soul mate amongst the animal kingdom? A friend of mine, a research scientist PhD from China, deeply loves her lap-dog. She takes the dog with her everywhere. She feeds him, while he perches on her thin legs, delicious delicacies off her plate. Still, my friend wants to fall in love with a guy, get married, and raise a family. No, I'm afraid one can't find a perfect soul mate in the animal kingdom any more than one can in the human kingdom—not completely, anyway.

Still, dog people know from experience that you can find a highly compatible dog that will love you loyally and deeply. The same I hold true for our meow friends. We should be able to bring to our lives a cat that we love and that loves us. No one knows exactly how many cats reside in the United States—so many are living wild in wood lots, dumps, and even college campuses—but one figure frequently suggested is seventy million. On the large campus of Texas A&M University, an organized group of faculty and staff works hard to get spayed legions of feral cats. Some of these cats have bloodlines going back generations; some are newly abandoned by students moving out of the dorms due to graduation or a return home for summer vacation.

On a half-forgotten street, in front of an old laboratory science building south of the campus's main Evans Library, a laminated sign with a colored photograph of an orange and white cat is attached to a stick mounted in low shrubbery. The sign reads, "This is Bisbee's place. Please do not feed or pet. Bisbee is well cared for." I've walked by the lab building a couple of times.

Now that I am not so financially impoverished, I could pick my next cat by its breed. Perhaps then personalities will be largely determined by genetics. The odds become more likely I'll be able to find a puss whose likes and dislikes correspond more closely to my likes and dislikes. Yes, somewhere out there, more than one true cat must be waiting. Or am I cursed forever to an ill fate? Can I ever acquire what it takes for the universe to see me worthy of a cat? Can my yearning ever lead to that special cat?

I hang on to hope. It may seem strange for a male of my generation, but I'm not so timid that I cannot to share feelings--

those negative, those positive. If I can raise my one true cat right, love the cat and care for the creature as best I can, then perhaps I can in a way atone for the cat who at the hospital fell from my arms to its death when I was four. Perhaps I can recover from the loss of Shogun in Japan to an early death, and from the loss of my dear cat of the woods, Skitzy. My dear friend and fellow poet Turquoise Woman up in Lamesa, Texas—sixty miles south of Lubbock—claims the kind of feline I hunger for does exist, but is rarer than a hard rain on the Texas panhandle during August. Most cats, she says, are "snobby" cats. They think they are too good for us.

"You want a cat that runs and jumps in your lap when you get home and purrs loudly whenever petted," Turquoise Woman says. "You want cat that sleeps with you at night. I've had maybe forty cats in my sixty-four years, but only two were like the kind you describe."

While at her house for a few hours on a trip to New Mexico, I'd been trying to pick up a blue-grey kitten I've spotted moving around Turquoise Woman's house. Her house overflows with life— all kinds of life—plants and pets and relatives and children. I am on my way to Santa Fe to look at property. Since a college student I've always wanted to live in an artist community of like-minded souls like Santa Fe. The little cat keeps slipping beyond my reach and finally slips behind a sofa.

I wish I had Turquoise Woman's skill at gathering life around me. If only, perhaps, I were more skilled in the kitchen? I look around and it seems so easy for women. I do know one gay man who can gather life that way. He is a superb cook.

Cats and dogs are the bridge to the wild kingdom from whence we came and remains a large part of us, always within us. Our animal selves, as well as our human selves, connect to the divine. I gain from my relation to the divine as expressed in the transcendent sky language of stars and heaven and God. I gain also from the

Buddhist principle of respect for all living things and find the divine as much in wild nature as in domesticated dogs and cats.

So divine are God's creatures to the Jain of India that their Saints continuously walk the country's rural paths naked saying prayers for the living. They are preceded by those who sweep the way with fallen peacock feathers. By these means, hopefully, the Jain saints will not step and crush any living creature, however small or seemingly insignificant.

I don't wish to belittle the divine that is not manifest, that is above and cannot be seen. Some call that divine the *mysterium tremendum* because our imaginations are paltry and fail in our heroic attempts to understand and picture what is beyond picturing or understanding. Wonderful therefore to have been given the divine in the material nearby that we can see and feel and smell and taste. Our senses are our windows to the world. Are they not in a way our first angels? The material divine, almost infinite in its variety, delights us daily because every day we come across something new we never could have imagined, not in a million years, like geckos scaling a sliding glass door.

We're having wild mushrooms tonight as part of our dinner. They are huge and marvelous, and the crowns of the mushrooms look like onion-flaked bagels. Our cats will eat their dry food tonight, dreaming of the moist tuna from the refrigerator in the morning.

With cats, for me at least, it all comes down to one of life's crucial journeys—the working out of one's practice of judgment, love, and forgiveness. It all comes down to a wrestling with the angels. Cats are the tack sticking up in the sole of my shoe. Thank you, cats, for being the irritant that has helped me learn about death, about living with others, about the necessary and hourly practice of forgiveness. I hear my wife yelling right now in the kitchen, "Dami, dami, no, no" at one of the cats.

Sayuri then comes and tells me that Stubby—the cat who spends much of her life inside—has made a kill. We've had her now six years.

"She is so proud!" Sayuri exclaims. "She brought it to the back door and left it as a birthday present for our daughter. Can you go bury it?"

"I guess so," I say. "Has Naomi admired the present?"

"Stubby was mewing at the door with her gift in her mouth," Sayuri exclaims again. "As soon as Naomi saw the sparrow Stubby dropped it and walked off." Our daughter's eighteenth birthday is in ten days.

Should I give up the search for the one true cat, and settle for happy imperfection that I'm dwelling in, a kind of cat polygamy?

I don't know. One can still hope. Life is long. I am an incurable dreamer, a lucky soul with seven grandchildren who has, God willing, fine years remaining. Tennyson's "Ulysses" was a favorite poem of my father's and a favorite of mine:

> Tho' much is taken, much abides; and though
> We are not now that strength which in old days
> Moved earth and heaven; that which we are, we are;
> One equal temper of heroic hearts,
> Made weak by time and fate, but strong in will
> > To strive, to seek, to find, and not to yield.

I am an ordinary soul, far from being an epic hero like Ulysses out of Homer's famous epic poem the *Odyssey*. Still, I'll continue to wrestle with the angels of life and seek the dream cat. Shots for rabies, long needles inserted in my stomach when I was a child in North Carolina, have failed to set me back for long. Our family has now lived in the same house for seventeen years. We seem to have established the needed income and stability to be successful with multiple cats, so perhaps, in spite of city codes that are rarely enforced, I can bring into our household a compatible, lap-loving, feline, or perhaps the right cat will show up at the door. Who knows? One thing I do know is that people will never understand the cat mind. There can be only cat minds, individual cats with distinct personalities. A person can with luck and perseverance, over time, begin to understand and love deeply one cat.

It's been about two years since I wrote the sentences above. Time flies—or does it flee? The year is 2012. The cat tree I told you about at the beginning still sits, unused and a bit dusty, on the ping pong table in the garage. I am in recovery from kidney cancer and surgery's complications. The days I spent in Texas' St. Joseph's hospital in July and August of 2011, lying in bed from the vagaries of surgery, remind me so much of the months in bed with asthma as a child in Illinois in 1949 and 1950.

As I now wind down this memoir, I look over at the little fellow who keeps me company during the day while my wife and daughter are at work. I've rearranged my work space so my little friend can be near but not on the floor. My friend is small and humans standing high above she finds intimidating. What happened next seems more than luck; it seems a miracle. Life can indeed be a church of happy surprises.

Love, we learn, involves not only luck but is a gradually acquired skill that includes perseverance. With luck and grace love may come and then you must continue always to practice, practice, practice this love. Love goes far beyond "being in love" and beyond deep feelings, although one can't dismiss those parts of love as unimportant. Love is an action verb, an activity you practice or carry out in the little things you do each day. No one offers you a fancy certificate and says OK, you are now a master of this course. Love means you are always learning how to love, and that makes love the greatest journey of our lives.

I will let our tortoise shell cat, Pounce, tell the rest of the story since the story belongs to her. What she shares is true, much more amazing than any writer's memories. These days the former hippie cat, the former "stoner" Pounce, does paw around on my laptop keyboard, but she does not claim to be an expert typist. What she has done instead is to *text* the rest of the story by way of a dream that arrived in my brain as I was in recovery from surgery.

See the next chapter.

24

For many years I was an outside cat. I came to this house in the midst of a raging thunderstorm, chased from my happy home by my own mother, at whose furry side I had nursed. I was chased away in a slanting rain but found shelter in the green van parked in a driveway. The sliding door was cracked open and I slipped inside to escape the wind and cold.

A few days later the man noticed me. I was frightened and hungry, yet he brought me water and food. I was skittish and stayed away from him. I had lost trust in the world, yet through the weeks he asked nothing of me and continued to bring food.

I soon realized that I was not the only cat of this realm. A tailless white and grey cat, who spent part of the day inside and part of the day outside, soon let me know she ruled this land and would have nothing to do with me. I was small, still the kitten, yet fending for myself. Dogs I heard roaming around at night, let loose by unthinking masters who did not consider the safety of others. Racoons and possums passed through in a hungry search for food. I was lucky I had the darkness of the green van to hide in.

The tailless cat would not let me in the backyard where she spent part of the day near a large golden dog. The dog did not mind cats, but the tailless would not tolerate me in the garage or the front yard. Luckily however, the cat seemed to accept that the driveway belonged to me. Perhaps the hard concrete was territory an inside cat would disdain, especially in summers when the Texas sun beats down.

About two months after I was chased from my litter a strange thing happened. Cats suddenly began to gather and hide in the bushes that ran up one side of the driveway. These cats were much larger than I and would croon their lonely songs at the night stars. A few nights the man inside the house dashed out carrying a flashlight to yell and chase the noisy cats away.

But one night these yelling cats came upon me. I thought at first that each one was going to tear me apart, but no, something else happened that I did not understand. Nine weeks later I gave birth to four baby kittens. I, who was not fully grown myself, found myself a mother. I was too small to nurse all these babies, but I did my best. Yes, I tried to be a good mother as I huddled with my kittens at the back of the van.

What happened to me next I can barely speak of. It tears my heart apart. In the stealth of night one of those big tomcats came. I fought with him briefly but it was impossible. He pushed me away and bit through the small furry heads of all my babies. The next day the man who fed opened the back van doors to check on the babies and me. When the sunlight poured in, there they were, curled up and dead.

The man blamed me. He shouted and I ran. He chased me up the driveway and for once I ducked under the crack at the bottom of the sliding garage door and hid in the dark behind a workbench. I was frightened but did not much blame the man. He did not know that a tom had come in the night.

The man who fed me kept feeding me but he had grown distant. He was grieving the death of the kittens. I understood that. The tailless cat seemed to accept my being in the garage now because the man was spending time there doing exercises on a machine. Tailless did not seem to like the man much. She preferred the lady of the house who gave her canned tuna. The rest of us cats, I eventually found out, were stuck with dried food.

The man would ride the exercise machine while watching the news on a small television perched on the work bench. I don't know why he liked the news so much because it was mostly about wars. I'd hear the sound of gunfire and it frightened me. I decided to forgive the man for blaming me for the terrible kitten deaths. It was an honest mistake.

So while the man rode the exercise machine I'd jump on the ping pong table, and then creep across the table near the net and try to climb on the man's lap. This was difficult because the man's legs were going up and down, but the upper part of his lap was fairly still. The man would pet me with one hand as he held onto the machine with the other.

I must admit being jealous that the man was not focused on me. I could have also used more food in my bowl, and so I did something I used to do when playing with my fellow kittens in the litter. I bit the man—gently I thought, playfully—on the flesh of his hand below his little finger. There seemed to be plenty of flesh on that spot, so I felt the nip would not hit a bone, or a nerve, or an artery.

Boy I was surprised by the man's response. He jumped off the exercise machine and shoved me from his lap. When my feet hit the cement of the garage floor, I dashed behind an old refrigerator kept in a corner. The man's hand was bleeding, I could tell from where I peered. My teeth must have broken through his skin. I was a kitten no more and did not know my own strength.

After the incident, the man continued to feed me but was even less friendly. He closed up the sliding door of the green van so I could not find shelter there, but he did leave an electric heater on in the garage for me to sleep by when the winter nights got below freezing. I spent most of my days somewhere on the driveway, sleeping on the top of a car, sleeping under a car, and on nights that were cold but not freezing, sleeping tucked next to the warm engine of a vehicle. I got to the engine by climbing up from under where things were open.

Years passed. I don't know how many because as a cat I do not keep a calendar. A third cat was now on the property, another young cat that just showed up one day as I did. The family in the house called him either Chibi or Chibe, and he was a wild sort of cat, a cat who caught and killed birds and small snakes. As he grew bigger and stronger, he began to quarrel with the tailless cat. One day in spring they got into a terrible rumble in the front yard where the dog could not reach them to break it up. Tailless won but her side was cut and bleeding. She had to spend a month in the house recuperating. I saw her on the carpet next to the sliding glass door. She acted so calm even when Chibi came up to the glass on the other side and put her two front paws up.

Chibi was so wild she would never even approach the food and milk bowls when they were filled. Tailless cat got well and the two continued to hiss, raise their backs, and scuffle. The dog continued to break them up. It was funny, peering out the garage door from under the ping pong table, to watch the dog charge, head down, between the cats, sending them scattering. They did not realize what a cream puff the dog was. Some nights I slept by his side, not quite touching, and he did not mind at all.

Time passed. I lived mostly on the driveway. In the dark shade under a car or the van I was unnoticed and often a breeze would funnel under. I got lucky one day and found that a vent window was unlocked and I worked it opened further using a paw. All I had to do from then on was make one leap up to the window and then slide inside the green van. I loved the cool silence of the van, loved my hiding place amongst stored Christmas lights, ornaments, and the old toys that belonged to the daughter who could not bear to throw them out. Sometimes, when getting out of his pickup, the man would stop to pet me as I lay in the sun. Daughter and madam began to stop and pet me too, although I was seen as the man's cat. I'd roll over and curl my paws, as I lay in the sun, in appreciation. They would scratch around my ears and under my chin.

But then one day Chibi drove the tailless cat away. We all expected Tailless to show up again after a couple of days. She had the run of many neighbor houses and had established a kind of food path from place to place. Tailless was a great leaper and had no trouble jumping to the top of the tall backyard fence. Chibi had a hole by the garage that she used to get out. I knew I was a small cat and felt safe where I was.

We all waited for Tailless to come back. The lady of the house was upset. The man who called Tailless by the name "Stubby" was not that upset. Daughter made a poster and taped copies of the poster on telephone poles all around the neighborhood. The man and the woman walked the neighborhood and went to the animal prison where pets who are not claimed are adopted out or killed. I heard the woman call the place the animal shelter and the man call it doggie Dachau. After a while I decided that Tailless must have had all she could take from Chibi and had found herself a safer place to live.

At last, we will be at peace around here, I thought, but I was wrong.

Chibi turned his attention on me and I was driven from the driveway to the front porch at the other end of the house. The lady put out a bamboo cat house she bought at a garage sale for me to sit and hide in. I tried to be as inconspicuous as possible. At times I hid in the sage bushes planted at the front of the house.

One time the man came home from work and found me at the side of the house, with back raised, hissing at Chibi, trying to drive her away. The man chased the wild cat back around the house to the garage. He yelled at Chibi to warn her off, saying that he would not tolerate Chibi driving off any more cats. The man petted me and walked over to the woman where she was pulling weeds in the yard. I followed because I knew he was my protector. Often I'd sit near the woman when she was working. I heard the man say, 'We will have to let the little one inside to prevent Chibi from driving her off.'

In? in? Inside!—where it was warm in winter, cool in summer, and I did not have to worry about racoons, possums, dogs, or the wild cat? I had at times felt the cool air rush out when the front door opened in summer, or the warm air in winter. I'd gotten in the habit of meowing at the front door and scratching in the door's corner when I was hungry. The family was no longer leaving extra food outside at night because the possum would raid the dish. Possum was getting brave. He even went in the garage now to get any food left for the dog or Chibi. I heard the man saying that we all needed to share the property with the possum because he was there before any humans moved in. The property was his land as much as it was our land.

Sometimes it was so cold that I would dash in the door when the man opened up to feed me. The big lightbulb they placed in my porch hut, by running a cord through the window, kept me warm at night—true—but I got tired of the light. More and more, I got to liking the notion of being inside. Sometimes I'd dash in and hide between boxes under a bed. Sometimes I'd hide upstairs. Always I would remember when I was a kitten in the litter and we cuddled together or played rough house. One day when I was inside the man was sitting on the living room sofa reading. The man likes books and the house is stuffed with them. I wonder if he eats books.

I don't know what I was thinking that early sunny winter afternoon as I sunned by the sliding glass door, but suddenly I found myself trotting across the carpet and jumping on the sofa two feet from him. He looked at me and seemed pleased. His hand reached over–tentatively–and began to stroke my fur. The way he did it showed he was worried I'd bite him. I started to purr loudly, pushing my head against his hand. The man started petting me with both hands. I got up and sat in his lap. I had to restrain myself from turning playful and taking a nip out of his hand. There's a spot on my backside that once touched seems to kick off an instinctive bite reaction in my brain. The man went back to reading and continued to stroke me, somewhat mechanically.

I was tempted to summon his thoughts back to me by taking a playful nip, but I resisted. I let him go on as he did and tried to accept what was given. The warm lap was nice if a bit bony. We sat together, the man and I, for a long while, and I could see the man was changed by the experience. He started calling me "kitten," "sweetheart," and other little endearing names. When he got up to fix tea in the kitchen, he set out more food for me. I was not hungry but took a few nibbles in appreciation.

The lady of the house was concerned. "This cat will bring fleas into the house," she said. "We don't want another flea invasion. I've already seen a few fleas jump off her." I could understand her concern. I did not like fleas either and tried to keep my fur clean by licking and biting whenever a flea attacked my skin.

The man got flea treatment and they held me down and put it under my fur, directly on my skin. I was frightened at first but have gotten used to the routine. I am a smart cat and without any help taught myself how to use the litter box, even though I don't care for the scratchy litter. Most of the time I get myself let out by meowing at the front door. I sit with the man because he seems to like it. I'll even play with the feather thing on a stick he waves in front of my face, although I know it's not a bird. He gets such a kick out of it.

I sit with the man much of the time. If he moves from the living room down the hall to the study or the bedroom, I will follow him. I can fully relax and get a good sleep when he's around. I was sitting with him last night while he made black marks on a piece of paper. He was on the sofa writing on a pad and I was curled up against him. The man has gotten good at pulling his hand away if he suspects I am about to take a nip. I am not quite sure why he doesn't like to play. He's much bigger than I and ought to be able to spare a few drops of blood. I sit with daughter too and with the lady of the house.

We love each other. They call me the one true cat. I appreciate that.

Pounce's Poem

I waited for them to love me
I waited in the rain under the eaves
I waited in the cold inside the van
I waited in the soaring heat of summer
    trying to catch a breeze in the shade
    under the pickup truck
I waited in the April sun playing
    with the waving puffballs of dandelions

I waited, worried about the sniffing dogs
    let out at night to wander
I waited, worried about the possum
    who lived in the hole by the fence
I waited, worried about wild cat twice
    my size who lived in back

Sometimes they would stop as I lay
    in the grass or on top of the car
sometimes he would sit in the grass
    and wiggle a twig in front of my nose
and I remember how they gave me
    shelter when my own mother drove
    me out from her love

I remember that first night in the van
    and the fierce slanting rain
I remember how the man fed me
    and so I waited through the years,
I waited for his love and for my turn,
    not counting time by the human way
but by the way of cats,
    a way of patient wisdom
outside of time...

I waited for love
    I waited and waited
I meowed at the door
    I scratched at the door
and then all of them, my family,
    opened the door
and let me in

As you can see, reader, I have become something of a literary cat by being around so many books and sitting on the laps of this household of readers. I try mewing at loud at times some of my own poetry. The man says cats have played a big part in human literature. He told me that Christopher Smart wrote a great poem about his cat Jeoffry, and that the beat cat, fiction writer Jack Kerouac, loved and wrote about his kitty Tyke, whose eyes were like the grass of autumn slitted with gold. In one of my other nine lives I must have been a bookstore cat.

I am however not modern but old fashioned—Victorian in my writing tastes—and believe good stories need to end with a moral.

My message to any humans who might happen to read this–and most of the four legged's know this instinctively–amounts to this: You know I am a cat, good at staying on my feet. Still, I fall and must get up. I waited years in the shadows before I found love.

Humans, be cat patient. Never give up.

You have more lives to live than you know.

BIOGRAPHICAL NOTE

Chuck Taylor has published two novels, *Drifter's Story* and *Fogg in High School*, as well as three short story collections, *Lights of the City, Somebody to Love,* and *It All Flows Away*.

His most recent books have been two poetry collections, *Like Li-Po Laughing at the Lonely Moon* and *At the Heart,* as well as a memoir, *Saving Sebastian: A Father's Journey through His Son's Drug Abuse*.

Taylor has worked as a bookstore clerk, children's magician, balloon clown, survey taker, janitor, soft water salesman, maintenance man, and animal lab assistant. He has also worked for in the National Endowment's CETA Artist Program, the Poets-in-the-School's Program, and taught at Angelo State University and the Universities of Texas at Tyler, El Paso, and Austin.

For over twenty years he has taught creative writing, film, American Nature Writing, and the Beat Movement in American Literature at Texas A&M University in College Station, Texas. He is married to Takako Saito and has three children, Will, James, and Lisa. He enjoys giving readings and writing workshops. He can be reached here:

theonetruecat@gmail.com

CPSIA information can be obtained at www.ICGtesting.com
Printed in the USA
LVOW121513181012

303458LV00009B/70/P